Contents

Foreword by the Translator i

An Introduction to Sūrah al-Najm v
Specifics of this Chapter v
Merits of Recitation viii

Part 1 11
The Great Oath - Verses 1-4 11
Thinking Points 11
Take Away Messages 16

Part 2 19
The Prophet - Verses 5-11 19
Thinking Points 19
Take Away Messages 24

Part 3 27
Will You Dispute? - Verses 12-15 27
Thinking Points 27
Take Away Messages 30

Part 4 33
The Major Signs - Verses 16-18 33
Thinking Points 33
Take Away Messages 34

Part 5 35
The Idols - Verses 19-22 35
Thinking Points 35
Take Away Messages 36

Part 6 39
Falsehood - Verse 23 39
Thinking Points 39
Take Away Messages 40

Part 7 41
The Authority - Verses 24-26 41
Thinking Points 41

A Review of the Concept of Aspirations in the Quran and *Aḥādīth* 44
The Significance of Having "Aspirations" 44
Restraining Our Aspirations 45
Negative Aspirations 45
Irresolvable Aspirations 46
Take Away Messages 47

Part 8 49
No Substitutes - Verses 27-28 49
Thinking Points 49
Take Away Messages 50

Part 9 51
The Paths - Verses 29-30 51
Thinking Points 51
Take Away Messages 54

Part 10 57
Infinite Justice - Verse 31 57
Thinking Points 57
Take Away Messages 58

Part 11 59
Vast Forgiveness - Verse 32 59
Thinking Points 59
Sins and the Disobedience of Allah ﷻ 64
Converting a Minor Sin to a Major Sin 66
Different Effects of Sins 66
How to Recompense for Sins 67
Take Away Messages 70

Part 12 73
The Deniers - Verses 33-37 73
Thinking Points 73
Take Away Messages 75

Part 13 79
What You Deserve - Verses 38-41 79
Thinking Points 79
Take Away Messages 83

بسم الله الرحمن الرحيم

In the Name of Allah,
the All-Compassionate,
the All-Merciful

Foreword by the Translator

From the multitudes of commentaries *(tafāsīr)* which have been written by Muslim scholars over the past 12 centuries in their attempts to better understand the Quran and make it relevant to the lives of every-day Muslims, the present work of Shaykh Muḥsin Qarā'atī, *Tafsīr Nūr - The Exegesis of Light*, is a unique attempt to bring the Quran into the homes of the Muslims.

Although sometimes very brief in his explanation, Shaykh Muḥsin makes up for the brevity of the commentary by providing the reader with **Take-Away Messages**. These detailed points guide the readers to key pieces of guidance on how to make the Quran relevant to their daily lives - thus, being able to *Live the Quran Through the Living Quran.*

We hope and pray that the translation and publication of this commentary serves to bridge the great divide which has existed within the Muslim community for generations and allows them to benefit from the beautiful teachings of the Noble Quran in their daily lives.

The initial project to translate *Tafsīr Nūr* into English was envisioned in early 2018, and initially was meant to strictly be a Podcast rendition of the translation.

However, due to popular demand and the support of well-wishers around the world, we expanded the scope of this project to release the PDF of the commentary of each chapter of the Quran as we completed them.

With the advancement in Print-On-Demand services globally, we have taken it a step further and decided to release the translation of the commentary of each chapter in print version.

The medium to long chapters of the Quran will be published in single books; while the shorter chapters of the Quran, such as those found in the 30th section *(juz')*, will be combined into books of manageable sizes.

Most commentaries of the Quran are published with each volume consisting of hundreds of pages, and this often puts some people off from wanting to try and understand the Quran. It is our hope that by publishing the commentary of the Quran in the format we have chosen - that is chapter by chapter - readers will be encouraged to pick up the exegesis of the chapter which interests them the most. In this way, over time, they will have read the commentary of the entire Quran, gaining inspiration from its teachings.

In closing, we are looking for lovers of the Quran to step forward to support this project by sponsoring its publication. Either individually or with your family, friends, and community members, choose a chapter of the Quran which you would like to see published, and contact us at iph@iph.ca. We will discuss the financial contribution required to cover translation, editing, and design work. In addition, the names of the donors or those whom they wish to dedicate the volume will be printed in the book for their Divine rewards.

In conclusion, we pray to Allah ﷻ to allow us to complete the translation of this brief, yet unique look into the Noble Quran, and that we can spread the beautiful teachings of Allah ﷻ through *Living the Quran Through the Living Quran.*

Saleem Bhimji
Director *of the* Islamic Publishing House

سورة النجم

An Introduction to Sūrah al-Najm

This sūrah is chapter number 53, has 62 verses, was revealed in Mecca, and is one of the chapters of the Quran which contains an obligatory prostration *(wājib sajdah)* within it.

The name of this chapter has been taken from its first verse in which Allah ﷻ takes an oath by the star.

There is a reference to the status of the Divine revelation *(waḥī)*, and the method by which the Quran was revealed to the heart of the Prophet ﷺ contained within this chapter. In addition, as seen in Sūrah al-Isrā' (17), there is also a mention about the night ascension to the heavens *(meʿrāj)* of the Noble Prophet ﷺ included in this chapter. Another portion of this chapter is regarding the superstitious beliefs of the disbelievers in their idols, and their worshipping of the angels, and in that vein they have been reprimanded for these beliefs and actions.

However, that which is the main thrust of this chapter is the focus on the Day of Judgement, and the state of the righteous doers and the evil individuals, and to know the criterion of the punishments and rewards of the Divine.

Specifics of this Chapter[1]

According to some scholars, this was the first entire chapter that was revealed to Prophet Muḥammad ﷺ after he began his open propagation of the message, and historians relate that he read this

---

[1] Extracted from *Tafsīr Nemunah.*

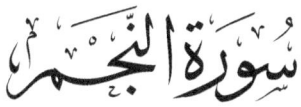

chapter aloud in Mecca in the Sacred Shrine *(Masjid al-Ḥarām).* Upon completing the recitation of this chapter, both the polytheists and the believers who heard him fell into prostration to Allah ﷻ.[2]

According to another group of commentators of the Quran, this chapter was revealed in the month of Ramaḍhān in the fifth year after the open appointment of the Prophet ﷺ.[3]

Some other commentators have stated that this was the first chapter revealed to the Prophet ﷺ which contained a verse that when read or heard, necessitates an obligatory prostration to Allah ﷻ.[4] However according to the well-known opinion which states that Sūrah al-ʿAlaq was revealed before this chapter, and the fact that Sūrah al-ʿAlaq also contains an obligatory prostration at the end of it, the opinion that Sūrah al-Najm was the first chapter revealed to the Prophet ﷺ to contain an obligatory prostration cannot be accurate.

In any case, since this chapter was revealed in Mecca, it contains discussions regarding the principle beliefs, especially that of Prophethood, and the Day of Judgement; and it is a chapter which employs a constant threat and warning to spiritually awaken the disbelievers.

The contents of this sūrah can be divided into seven categories:

1. After the meaningful oaths taken by Allah ﷻ, the beginning of this chapter clearly speaks about the reality of the revelation, and the direct communication which the Prophet ﷺ had with the conveyor of this revelation, the

---

[2] *Tafsīr Rūḥ al-Bayān*, Vol. 9, Pg. 208.

[3] Ibid.

[4] *Tafsīr Murāghī*, Vol. 28, Pg. 41.

angel Jibrāʾīl ◈, and the fact that the sanctified Prophet ﷺ speaks nothing other than Divine revelations.

2. In another portion of this chapter, the night ascension *(meʿrāj)* of the Prophet ﷺ has been discussed, and a portion of the journey has been conveyed through the usage of short, yet very meaningful verses - and this discussion has a direct relationship with that of the Divine revelation *(waḥī)*.

3. The third portion of this chapter deals with some of the superstitions of the polytheists regarding their idols, their worshipping of the angels, and other issues which all stemmed from the following of their whims and desires. All these incorrect beliefs and practices of theirs have been rebuked, and they are warned that they should not be worshipping such things, and this is further proven through the usage of strong logical proofs.

4. In the next portion of this chapter, Allah ◈ shows the misguided individuals and the sinners the way to turn back to Him in repentance and reminds them that the doors of pardon are open for them. In addition, they are given the glad tidings of a 'spacious forgiveness.' A point of importance has been further emphasized regarding the fact that every single person is responsible for their own actions, and no one can carry the weight of the sins of another person on their shoulders.

5. To complete the goals of this chapter, in the fifth portion, a brief discussion on the issue of the resurrection is brought up, and clear proofs for this belief are presented by relying on what can be seen in the creation of this world and what exists therein.

6. In the sixth section, as is usually seen in the Quran, there are some points mentioned regarding the painful outcomes of the previous generations who took an adversarial approach to the truth and were rebellious and obstinate (such as the nations of ʿĀd, Thamūd, Nūḥ ﷺ, and Lūṭ ﷺ) so that those who have fallen into spiritual heedlessness *(ghaflah)* can be woken up.
7. Finally, the last portion of this chapter deals with the command to prostrate before Allah ﷻ and engage in worshipping Him.

One of the unique qualities of this chapter is that it contains short, yet immensely powerful verses which can have a deep impact on an individual, can awaken the sleeping heart and soul, and spiritually elevate a person higher up towards the heavens.

Merits of Recitation[5]

Regarding the merits of recitation of this *sūrah*, the traditions mention the following:

In a *ḥadīth* from Prophet Muḥammad ﷺ, he says:

مَنْ قَرَأَ سُورَةَ وَالنَّجْمِ أُعْطِيَ مِنَ الْأَجْرِ عَشْرَ حَسَنَاتٍ بِعَدَدِ مَنْ صَدَّقَ بِمُحَمَّدٍ وَمَنْ جَحَدَ بِهِ.

"A person who recites Sūrah al-Najm will be given a reward of ten good deeds *(ḥasanāt)* for every person who believed in Muḥammad, and for every person who disputed with him."[6]

---

[5] Extracted from *Tafsīr Nemunah.*

[6] *Tafsīr Majmaʿ al-Bayān*, Vol. 9, Pg. 175.

In another *ḥadīth*, this one from Imām Jaʿfar ibn Muḥammad al-Ṣādiq ﷺ, we read:

مَنْ كَانَ يُدْمِنُ قِرَاءَةَ وَالنَّجْمِ فِي كُلِّ يَوْمٍ أَوْ فِي كُلِّ لَيْلَةٍ عَاشَ مَحْمُودًا بَيْنَ النَّاسِ وَكَانَ مَوْفُورًا لَهُ وَ كَانَ مَحْبُوبًا بَيْنَ النَّاسِ.

"A person who is habituated to reciting (Sūrah) al-Najm every day or every night will live a blessed life among the people, will be forgiven for their sins, and will gain the affection of the people in society."[7]

Without a doubt, such grand rewards are for the person who recites, reflects, and ponders on this *sūrah* of the Quran, then acts (righteously), and tries to put the various teachings of this chapter into practice in one's daily life.

[7] *Biḥār al-Anwār*, Vol. 92, Pg. 305.

Part 1

The Great Oath - Verses 1-4

بِسۡمِ ٱللَّهِ ٱلرَّحۡمَٰنِ ٱلرَّحِيمِ

In the Name of Allah, the All-Compassionate, the All-Merciful

وَٱلنَّجۡمِ إِذَا هَوَىٰ ١ مَا ضَلَّ صَاحِبُكُمۡ وَمَا غَوَىٰ ٢ وَمَا يَنطِقُ عَنِ ٱلۡهَوَىٰٓ ٣ إِنۡ هُوَ إِلَّا وَحۡيٞ يُوحَىٰ ٤

1. By the star as it goes down.

2. Your companion (Muḥammad) has not gone astray, nor has he erred.

3. Nor does he speak out of (his own) desire.

4. It is nothing but a revelation revealed.

Thinking Points

The word *'hawā'* refers to 'a tendency to fall down;' thus the term '*hawā al-nafs*' - 'the lower desires' are 'those demands of the base aspects of the soul which cause a person to metaphorically slip or fall down.'

The word *'ḍhalla'* refers to 'being misguided from the Straight Path;' and the word *'ghawā'* refers to 'a deviation in beliefs whose roots lie in false theological principles.'

The word *'ṣāḥib'* refers to 'a friend and helper,' and this word has been used multiple times in the Quran regarding the Prophet of Islam ﷺ[8] because the interactions of the Prophet ﷺ with the people were built upon closeness, compassion, and rooted in friendliness.

It is interesting to note that the last word of the previous chapter (Sūrah al-Ṭūr) was *'nujūm'* or 'stars' (the plural form of the word), and the first word of this chapter is *'najm'* or 'star' (the singular form of the word).

The meaning of the verse which reads 'By the star as it goes down' is either the time of sunrise every morning in which the radiance of the stars loses their luminosity [due to the brightness of the sun], or it may refer to the time at the end of this world and the beginning of the Day of Judgement when the stars will completely collapse.

When it comes to the teachings of Monotheism *(Tawḥīd)*, Allah ﷻ and His Prophet ﷺ act to verify one another. Allah ﷻ absolves His Prophet ﷺ from all forms of deviation, just as He says in the second verse of this chapter: "Your friend (Muḥammad) has not gone astray, nor has he erred."

At the same time, the Prophet ﷺ also cleared any misgivings which the people may have had about Allah ﷻ.[9]

---

[8] Quran, Sūrah Saba' (34), verse 46; Sūrah al-A'rāf (7), verse 184; and Sūrah al-Takwīr (81), verse 22.

[9] Although the pre-Islamic Arabs who lived in the Arabian Peninsula at one point had been monotheists and had the honour of being the custodians of the first house of worship built for humanity, the Ka'bah, which Prophets Ibrāhīm ؑ and Ismā'īl ؑ constructed, gradually they went towards polytheism.

Through the Quran and the guidance of Prophet Muḥammad ﷺ, the mindset of the pagan Arabs was shifted, allowing them to have a correct understanding of the One True God - Allah ﷻ.

When introducing the Quran, Allah ﷻ says: "That is the Book in which there is no doubt..."[10]

At the same time, when speaking about His Prophet ﷺ, He says: "Nor does he speak out of desire."

This has been done to close all possibilities of people launching any accusations against Allah ﷻ and His Prophet ﷺ, and so that no doubts may remain in their hearts.

Below are three examples in how the teachings of Islam, as inspired by the Quran, sought to change the mindset of the pre-Islamic Arabs, and give them the true understanding of Allah ﷻ:

1. The Quran attests many times that the polytheistic Arabs "believed" in Allah ﷻ as God, however alongside that, they also worshipped thousands of other "gods." Thus, they created "gods" for phenomena such as rain, a massive harvest, love, etc. Prophet Muḥammad ﷺ was successful in getting most of these individuals to leave polytheism and dedicate themselves to the One True God - Allah ﷻ - recognizing that He is the source of everything that occurs.

2. When slaughtering an animal, they would dedicate the food and blood to their "gods" - thinking that the statutes they worshipped wanted this, thus this was another area where Prophet Muḥammad ﷺ and the Quran were able to change their understanding in regards to.

3. The pre-Islamic Arabs regarded the angels as the daughters of Allah ﷻ which is mentioned numerous times in the Quran, and this is yet another area where Prophet Muḥammad ﷺ worked hard to make his community understand that this was incorrect.

The pre-Islamic Arabs believed these and many other incorrect things about Allah ﷻ which had to slowly be eradicated from their psyche and replaced with the correct understanding of the Oneness of Allah ﷻ. (Tr.)

[10] Quran, Sūrah al-Baqarah (2), verse 2:

﴿ذَٰلِكَ الْكِتَابُ لَا رَيْبَ فِيهِ...﴾

Allah ﷻ rebukes those who went astray and says to them: You were friends and companions of the Prophet ﷺ for a long period of time, and you know fully well that he is **not** a deviant! The Quran says: "Your friend (Muḥammad) has not gone astray, nor has he erred."

The unique qualities of the leaders who were appointed by the Divine over those who are appointed by the people can be summarized into the following:

The leaders that are deputed by Allah ﷻ:

1. Do not have any history of mental deviation.
2. They do not have any background of sins or immorality in their past.
3. Have compassion and empathy for the people.
4. Have never allowed their own lower desires and passions, or that of others to overcome them [making them do wrong thing in life].

The late Shaykh Ṣadūq ؒ in his book, *al-Amālī*, when speaking about the fact that a person can never please everyone, and that peoples' tongues cannot be controlled has stated: "There are some people who consider even someone like the Noble Prophet ﷺ as being one who is under the influence of his lower desires and passions, so in response to this Allah defended His Prophet and says: 'Nor does he speak out of [his own] desire.'"[11]

We read in a *ḥadīth* that Ḥamzah, the uncle of the Noble Prophet ﷺ, once asked the Prophet ﷺ: "Why is it that all of the doors of the *Masjid* (in Medina) which were previously open [the houses which were adjacent to the *Masjid* had back doors which opened into the *Masjid* making it easy for people to come out of their houses and go straight into the *Masjid*, rather than having to

---

[11] *Al-Amālī* of Shaykh Ṣadūq.

go through their front door and then make their way to the entrance of the *Masjid*] have all been closed off except for the door of ʿAlī ﷺ?" To this question, the Prophet ﷺ recited the first few verses of Sūrah al-Najm and said: 'It is but a revelation revealed' - meaning that everything the Prophet ﷺ did was in total obedience to the commands of Allah ﷻ.[12]

In addition, when Imam ʿAlī ﷺ was appointed to the position of leadership and the successor of the Prophet ﷺ during the event of Ghadīr al-Khumm, Prophet Muḥammad ﷺ was criticized by those around him, thus in response the Prophet ﷺ merely responded by reciting this verse of the Quran where Allah ﷻ says: 'It is but a revelation revealed.'[13]

In response to the disbelievers who used to say 'This [Quran] is nothing but stories from the former people,'[14] Allah ﷻ categorically responded to them by saying 'It is but a revelation revealed.'

The Quran is **not** a book of poetry, and its verses *(āyāt)* do not follow the rules of how poetry is composed. However, from the point of view of its unique arrangement in the words and statements, the pleasure a person gets from reciting and hearing it, and the way it can be recited - it is sheer beauty and balanced just

---

[12] *Tafsīr al-Durr al-Manthūr.*

[13] *Tafsīr Nūr al-Thaqalayn.*

[14] Quran, Sūrah al-Anʿām (6), verse 25:

﴿وَمِنْهُم مَّن يَسْتَمِعُ إِلَيْكَ ۖ وَجَعَلْنَا عَلَىٰ قُلُوبِهِمْ أَكِنَّةً أَن يَفْقَهُوهُ وَفِىٓ ءَاذَانِهِمْ وَقْرًا ۚ وَإِن يَرَوْا۟ كُلَّ ءَايَةٍ لَّا يُؤْمِنُوا۟ بِهَا ۚ حَتَّىٰٓ إِذَا جَآءُوكَ يُجَـٰدِلُونَكَ يَقُولُ ٱلَّذِينَ كَفَرُوٓا۟ إِنْ هَـٰذَآ إِلَّآ أَسَـٰطِيرُ ٱلْأَوَّلِينَ ٢٥﴾

like some styles of poetry are. This is better seen by the last words in these four verses:

1. *Hawā*
2. *Ghawā*
3. *al-Hawā*
4. *Yūḥā*

Take Away Messages

1. A person can even take an oath by the creations which are seen in nature because these are all signs of Allah ﷻ.
2. The motion of the stars is towards destruction and collapse, and without a doubt, in the future they will face this fate.
3. There are many slanders which a person will come across from others in the way of propagating the religion, however Allah ﷻ is always there to defend the sincere ones.
4. The Prophets (AS) spent their lives among the deviant people of society; however, they did not allow themselves to become corrupt, and this is one more sign of their greatness.
5. The great skies will eventually be destroyed; however, the Prophets (AS) and their words will remain immutable.
6. The commands and words of the Prophet ﷺ are a proof over us and are a binding upon us to listen to and obey.
7. The Noble Prophet ﷺ was not deviant in the past, nor will he ever deviate in the future.
8. The higher the authority and responsibility becomes for a person, the greater the guarantee of the safeguarding of

that person's [mental and spiritual] well-being will be from Allah ﷻ.

9. In principles of management, those people who are virtuous must be defended, and all accusations against them must be countered.
10. The Prophet ﷺ himself is on the path of truth and so are his words.
11. The words of the Prophet ﷺ did not come from his own personal desires, nor from the social environment in which he lived, rather they were revelations from the Almighty ﷻ.
12. The decision to send down revelations *(waḥī)* and their content, time, place, and quantity are all in the authority of Allah ﷻ.
13. The lower desires and passions are not compatible with revelations.

Part 2

The Prophet - Verses 5-11

عَلَّمَهُۥ شَدِيدُ ٱلْقُوَىٰ ﴿٥﴾ ذُو مِرَّةٍ فَٱسْتَوَىٰ ﴿٦﴾ وَهُوَ بِٱلْأُفُقِ ٱلْأَعْلَىٰ
﴿٧﴾ ثُمَّ دَنَا فَتَدَلَّىٰ ﴿٨﴾ فَكَانَ قَابَ قَوْسَيْنِ أَوْ أَدْنَىٰ ﴿٩﴾ فَأَوْحَىٰٓ إِلَىٰ
عَبْدِهِۦ مَآ أَوْحَىٰ ﴿١٠﴾ مَا كَذَبَ ٱلْفُؤَادُ مَا رَأَىٰٓ ﴿١١﴾

5. Taught to him by one intense in strength,

6. The one of vigour, and he rose,

7. While he was at the highest (part of the) horizon.

8. Then he approached and came down.

9. Then He was within two bows' length, or closer.

10. Then He revealed to His servant what He revealed.

11. The heart did not lie about what it saw.

Thinking Points

The word '*mirra*' means 'something which is twisted together,' and it could also be in the meaning of 'strong.' Thus, this word is sometimes used in the meaning of 'power and strength.' We see this usage in a *ḥadīth* from the Messenger of Allah ﷺ regarding charity *(ṣadaqah)* in which he has been quoted as saying that this is something which he called *'mirra'* and *'sawwī'* - meaning that 'charity is not for those who are wealthy.'[15]

The word *danā* means 'going close,' however the word *tadallā* means 'going extremely close' such that due to the extreme closeness, those things are connected. The word *qāba* is close in meaning to the word 'measure,' and the word *qaws* means an arc, thus the phrase *qāba qawsayn* is an allusion to the extreme level of proximity that the Prophet ﷺ was to Allah ﷻ at the time of the revelation *(waḥī)*.

Scholars of the Quran have debated the meaning of *Shadīd al-Quwā* and whether it refers to Allah ﷻ or to angel Jibrā'īl. When this phrase appears in other places, it refers solely to Allah ﷻ. For example, in *Du'ā al-Nudbah*, we read: "And grant one (Your servant) the chance to see one's master (meaning Imam al-Zamān or Imam al-Ḥujjah), O the Lord of Mighty Prowess."[16]

Or in one of the supplications that has been narrated from Imam al-Ḥasan which is beneficial for warding off the evil of oppressors, we read: "O the Lord of Mighty Prowess, O the Lord of a Mighty Punishment."[17]

In addition to this, in other verses of the Quran, Allah ﷻ refers to Himself as the Teacher of the Quran, for example in Sūrah al-Raḥmān we read: "The Beneficent God, He taught the Quran."[18]

---

[15] *Tafsīr Rūḥ al-Ma'ānī.*

[16] The Arabic of this is as follows:

وَأَرِهِ سَيِّدَهُ يَا شَدِيدَ الْقُوَى

[17] *Mustadrak al-Wasā'il*, Vol. 5, Pg. 260:

يَا شَدِيدَ الْقُوَى يَا شَدِيدَ الْمِحَالِ

[18] Quran, Sūrah al-Raḥmān (55), verse 1:

"And He taught you what you did not know."[19]

Of course, it must be noted that in Sūrah al-Takwīr we see that when speaking about the angel Jibrā'īl ﷺ, he has been called: "(The) possessor of strength"[20]

However, there is a huge difference between '*dhī quwwa*' - 'possessor of strength' and '*shadīd al-quwā*' - 'intense in strength;' therefore we can state that the meaning of '*shadīd al-quwā*' is none other than Allah ﷻ Himself.

In these verses under review, the issue of the ascension *(me'rāj)* of the Prophet ﷺ has been referred to, and those wishing to know more about this event can refer to the event of *me'rāj* discussed in volume 7 of *Tafsīr Nūr* which reviews the first verse of Surah al-Isrā'.

In *Tafsīr Rūḥ al-Ma'ānī* it has been stated that: "During the time of the Age of Ignorance *(Jāhiliyyah)* when two people wanted to establish close ties between themselves, they would [stand beside one another and] put their bows alongside themselves, then pull the string of their bows together at the same time, both shooting arrows - and this was symbolic of the two of them becoming very close."

In the explanation of these verses, it must be noted that it is not the angel who was on the highest horizon *(al-ufuq al-a'lā)*, rather

---

﴿ٱلرَّحْمَٰنُ ۝١ عَلَّمَ ٱلْقُرْءَانَ ۝٢﴾

[19] Quran, Sūrah al-Nisā' (4), verse 113:

﴿...وَعَلَّمَكَ مَا لَمْ تَكُن تَعْلَمُ...﴾

[20] Ibid., Sūrah al-Takwīr (81), verse 20:

﴿ذِى قُوَّةٍ...﴾

the angel was in the clear horizon *(al-ufuq al-mubīn)*, and it was the Prophet ﷺ who was at a much higher level (than the angel), and it was him who was able to witness the angel, as Allah ﷻ says: 'And certainly he (meaning the Prophet) saw him (the angel) in the clear horizon.'[21]

Allah ﷻ does not reside in a physical location, therefore the meaning of the phrase the highest horizon *(al-ufuq al-aʿlā)* is not a specific geographic location - rather it refers to Him being at the highest pinnacle of Greatness and is an allusion to Allah's ﷻ over-arching Awareness and Authority over everything.

When on the Earth, revelation *(waḥī)* happens through intermediaries: "The Faithful Spirit has descended with it, upon your (Muḥammad ﷺ) heart."[22]

Angel Jibrāʾīl (a) was the one who brought down the Quran to the heart of the Prophet ﷺ; however, when the discussion changes to that of the *meʿrāj* of the Prophet ﷺ, then Allah ﷻ changes the words and says: "And He (meaning Allah ﷻ) revealed to His servant what He revealed." This means that when it comes to the station of extreme spiritual proximity, there is absolutely no room for an intermediary, and even the closest of angels are not permitted to be involved in such an encounter.

It was once asked of Imam al-Sajjād (a): "What is the rationale behind the *meʿrāj* of the Noble Prophet ﷺ?! Does Allah have a physical location?" The Imam (a) replied: "The *meʿrāj* was because

---

[21] Quran, Sūrah al-Takwīr (81), verse 23:

﴿وَلَقَدْ رَءَاهُ بِٱلْأُفُقِ ٱلْمُبِينِ ﴿٢٣﴾﴾

[22] Ibid., Sūrah al-Shuʿarāʾ (26), verses 193-194:

﴿نَزَلَ بِهِ ٱلرُّوحُ ٱلْأَمِينُ ﴿١٩٣﴾ عَلَىٰ قَلْبِكَ...﴾

Allah wanted to show His Prophet whatever is contained within the expanses of the skies, and all that is there from the amazing creations and workings."[23]

The lessons that the Prophet ﷺ attained in the *meʿrāj* were specific learnings, some of which include the following:

1. A 'classroom' setting is the best place to learn as Allah ﷻ says 'When he was in the highest part of the horizon.'
2. The 'teacher' in this class (Allah ﷻ) was the strongest of all teachers, as Allah ﷻ says 'Taught to him by one intense in strength.'
3. The content of what was being learned (revelation) was the strongest of things which can be taught, as Allah ﷻ says 'That (which the Prophet ﷺ conveys to you) is but a Revelation that was revealed to him.'

One of the immaculate Imams ﵇ was once asked: "Did the Messenger of Allah see His Lord (on the *meʿrāj*)?" The Imam ﵇ replied: "Yes, He saw him with the eyes of his heart."

The Imam ﵇ then went on to recite this verse of Sūrah al-Najm in which Allah ﷻ says: "The heart did not contradict what it saw (with his eyes)."

In addition, Imam al-Riḍā ﵇ has been quoted as saying that the verse: "Indeed, he saw (one) among the greatest signs of His Lord"[24] explains verse 11 of this chapter which reads: "The heart did not contradict what it saw (with his eyes)." This means that the understanding of 'seeing' in this verse is 'seeing the **signs** of Allah ﷻ' - NOT the Essence of Allah ﷻ.

---

[23] *Tafsīr Kanz al-Daqāʾiq.*

[24] Quran, Sūrah al-Najm (53), verse 18.

Take Away Messages

1. Religion *(dīn)* is such a valuable thing that its teacher must be none other than Allah ﷻ, as He is the **only** One who is limitless in His Power; and the student cannot be anyone other than the Prophet ﷺ himself as he, along with the 13 select members of his family (the Ahlul Bayt ﷺ), are the only ones who are completely free from any blunders or slips, and are truly immaculate in every sense.
2. Benefitting from the Divine teachings require an individual to have an exceptional capacity of receptivity.
3. One of the ways to know the true character of a person is by knowing who their teacher is.
4. Revelation *(waḥī)* is like Divine teaching and schooling.
5. Clear responses must be given to false accusations - in reply to those who used to say that others have taught the Prophet ﷺ this Quran - 'only a mortal teaches him,'[25] Allah ﷻ responds by saying - 'The Lord of Mighty Power taught him.'
6. The Prophet's ﷺ knowledge came directly from Allah ﷻ.
7. The Knowledge *('Ilm)* of the Divine is not separate from His Power *(Qudrah)*.
8. It is **only** Allah ﷻ who is the incredibly Powerful One, and all others who claim power are weak.
9. Through the instructions and teachings of Allah ﷻ, one (meaning Prophet Muḥammad ﷺ) who was considered as

[25] Quran, Sūrah al-Naḥl (16), verse 103:

﴿وَلَقَدْ نَعْلَمُ أَنَّهُمْ يَقُولُونَ إِنَّمَا يُعَلِّمُهُۥ بَشَرٌ لِّسَانُ ٱلَّذِى يُلْحِدُونَ إِلَيْهِ أَعْجَمِىٌّ وَهَٰذَا لِسَانٌ عَرَبِىٌّ مُّبِينٌ ﴿١٠٣﴾﴾

an '*ummī*' (one who never went to a formal school to take in knowledge) can become a teacher for all of humanity.

10. All human beings are general students of Allah ﷻ - 'He (Allah ﷻ) taught the human being that which he knew not;'[26] however it is only the Prophet ﷺ himself who was a 'special' student of Allah ﷻ - 'The Lord of Mighty Power taught him.'
11. The training program of the Divine for humanity is something which is robust and complete.
12. Closeness to Allah ﷻ comes about gradually - step by step.
13. The relationship between a teacher and a student must be a close, personal bond.
14. When speaking, a person must make use of the words and styles of the audience, and one needs to speak to the people in their 'language.' Allah ﷻ says in this passage that the Prophet ﷺ came two bow lengths or closer - in mentioning this, we see that in the culture of the Arabs, when two people had 'their bows which are close to one another' this was a symbol of the closeness of those two individuals (who owned the bows), so Allah ﷻ used similar language for them to better understand such concepts.
15. There is no limit to the level of proximity which can be attained between Allah ﷻ and a servant of His - and this is something which the angels will never be able to attain.
16. The people of Allah ﷻ - whether they be on the Earth or in the heavens are still servants of the Almighty ﷻ - as in the

---

[26] Quran, Sūrah al-ʿAlaq (96), verse 5:

﴿عَلَّمَ ٱلْإِنسَٰنَ مَا لَمْ يَعْلَمْ ۝٥﴾

case of the *meʿrāj* in which Allah ﷻ said '(who took) **His servant** to go on a Night Journey.'[27]

17. Servitude to Allah ﷻ is the platform through which a person can gain inspiration and Divine blessings.
18. The Noble Prophet ﷺ was free of any sins or mistakes when it came to receiving the revelation *(waḥī)* and in conveying it.
19. The inner-witnessing *(shuhūd al-bāṭinī)* is an evidence *(ḥujjat)* which Allah ﷻ Himself has confirmed.

[27] Quran, Sūrah al-Isrāʾ (17), verse 1:

﴿سُبْحَٰنَ ٱلَّذِىٓ أَسْرَىٰ بِعَبْدِهِۦ لَيْلًا مِّنَ ٱلْمَسْجِدِ ٱلْحَرَامِ إِلَى ٱلْمَسْجِدِ ٱلْأَقْصَا ٱلَّذِى بَٰرَكْنَا حَوْلَهُۥ
لِنُرِيَهُۥ مِنْ ءَايَٰتِنَآ ۚ إِنَّهُۥ هُوَ ٱلسَّمِيعُ ٱلْبَصِيرُ ١﴾

Part 3

Will You Dispute? - Verses 12-15

أَفَتُمَٰرُونَهُۥ عَلَىٰ مَا يَرَىٰ ﴿١٢﴾ وَلَقَدۡ رَءَاهُ نَزۡلَةً أُخۡرَىٰ ﴿١٣﴾ عِندَ سِدۡرَةِ
ٱلۡمُنتَهَىٰ ﴿١٤﴾ عِندَهَا جَنَّةُ ٱلۡمَأۡوَىٰٓ ﴿١٥﴾

12. Will you dispute with him concerning what he saw?

13. And surely, he saw him on another descent,

14. At the Lotus Tree of the extremity (utmost boundary).

15. Near which is the Garden of Abode.

Thinking Points

The word '*tumārūnahu*' comes from the word '*maraa*'' and refers to 'argumentation accompanied with doubts and misgivings;' the word '*nazlah*' refers to 'something being sent down in one instance;' the term '*Sidratul Muntahā*' refers to 'a physical location near the promised Paradise which is full of the graces of the Divine,' and according to the traditions, no one other than the Prophet of Islam ﷺ has traversed past that point.[28]

It has been mentioned in a tradition: "That location which is the final stage where the angels can ascend to is known as the final station where good actions can reach, and that place is known as *Sidratul Muntahā.*"

---

[28] *Tafsīr Kanz al-Daqā'iq.*

We also read in the traditions that: "*Sidratul Muntahā* is the name of a tree, and for as many leaves as there are on this tree, there is an angel assigned to each leaf whose responsibility is to glorify Allah ﷻ (engage in His *tasbīḥ*)."[29]

Since there are a lot of doubts and disbeliefs regarding the event of *meʿrāj*, in the very first verse of Sūrah al-Isrāʾ, Allah ﷻ proclaims: "Glory be to Him." By saying this, Allah ﷻ wants humankind to know that He is free from doing any frivolous actions, and that the *meʿrāj* had a lofty goal to it.

In the chapter we are currently reviewing, Allah ﷻ poses a question by asking us in verse 12: "Will you dispute with him concerning what he saw?"

By Allah ﷻ speaking about the *meʿrāj* in this form, He is once again trying to get the people to remove any doubts or disbeliefs they may harbour about this event. In essence, Allah ﷻ is saying that if we believe in Prophet Muḥammad ﷺ and what he does and says to us, then we should not dispute with the Prophet ﷺ regarding what he experienced on the *meʿrāj* as the Muslims have already come to trust him and all of his previous statements.

Although every human being is under the supervision of Allah ﷻ, sometimes the Almighty One 'glances' towards some individuals in a special fashion, as we read: "And surely He saw him on another descent." By saying this, Allah ﷻ is in fact noting that on the *meʿrāj* of His Prophet ﷺ, He glanced at His Prophet ﷺ in a unique way.

---

[29] *Tafsīr Nemunah* and *Tafsīr Majmaʿ al-Bayān.*

This same thing can be seen in other verses of the Quran such as when Allah ﷻ says that He is with all people: "And He is with you all."[30]

However, Allah's ﷻ "being with" those who have God-consciousness *(taqwā)* is a unique type of "being with" as He says: "Indeed Allah is with those people who have God-consciousness."[31]

Thus, sometimes the state of 'being' with someone and the graces of Allah ﷻ are of a general nature, while other times it is of a more specific type. The Almighty ﷻ took His Prophet ﷺ into the heavens as a guest, brought him to an area known as *Sidratul Muntahā* and the promised Paradise, and gave him this very special treatment.[32]

However, in other commentaries of the Quran, it has been stated that: "On another occasion, the Prophet ﷺ saw [angel] Jibrā'īl عليه السلام in his original form and substance;" or [as stated in another commentary]: "The Prophet ﷺ saw Allah ﷻ with his [the Prophet's] inner vision."

The reason why we have chosen to accept the statement found in *Tafsīr Aṭyab al-Bayān* is that these verses of the Quran are elevating the greatness of the Prophet ﷺ and his journey of the *me'rāj;* but the act of seeing Jibrā'īl عليه السلام - keeping in mind that the status of the Prophet ﷺ is much higher than that of Jibrā'īl عليه السلام -

---

[30] Quran, Sūrah al-Ḥadīd (57), verse 4:

﴿...وَهُوَ مَعَكُمْ أَيْنَ مَا كُنتُمْ...﴾

[31] Ibid., Sūrah al-Naḥl (16), verse 128:

﴿إِنَّ ٱللَّهَ مَعَ ٱلَّذِينَ ٱتَّقَوا۟...﴾

[32] *Tafsīr Aṭyab al-Bayān.*

would not really be considered as an honour or some exaltation of the Prophet ﷺ, thus it does not fit with the style of these verses.

In addition, the Prophet ﷺ witnessing Allah ﷻ with the inner vision is something which was always available for the Prophet ﷺ and did not occur just once or twice. However, the special grace of Allah ﷻ in the event of the *meʿrāj* is something which was given special attention because Allah ﷻ brought His Prophet ﷺ on this journey into the heavens for a special reason. He glanced at His Prophet ﷺ with a special look - as Allah ﷻ says: "And surely he saw him on another descent."

In the traditions we read that the Messenger of Allah ﷺ said: "I saw Jibrāʾīl near the *Sidratul Muntahā* and he said to me: 'The last point which Allah has allowed me to traverse is this point right here, and if I go any forward, then my wings will be burnt.'"[33]

Take Away Messages

1. Those who have no faith *(īmān)* do not have the ability to accept the spiritual revelations *(mukāshifāt)* and that which is granted to the close friends *(awliyāʾ)* of Allah ﷻ, therefore such people will seek to enter disputation and cast doubts on those individuals who are blessed to have these experiences.
2. Regarding theoretical and intellectual issues which come up, there is room for discussion and possibly some area of doubt, however when it comes to that which is seen, then there is no room for disputes or misgivings. Generally speaking, if two people see the exact same thing, they

---

[33] *Tafsīr Hidāyah.*

should be able to offer similar statements on what they saw.

3. One of the outcomes of propagation is that not everyone will accept what is being said automatically - there will always be people who deny, have doubts, and enter into dispute.
4. Asking questions and seeking proofs is something which has always been recommended in our faith as the Quran says: 'So ask the people of the reminder...;'[34] however when it comes to argumentation and confrontation, these are things which have been chided.
5. There are things which are even greater than Paradise - just as Allah ﷻ says: 'At the Lotus Tree of the extremity, Near which is the Garden of Abode' - the tree known as *Sidratul Muntahā* is so important that Paradise, with all of its greatness, has been mentioned alongside it.

[34] Quran, Sūrah al-Naḥl (16), verse 43:

﴿...فَسْـَٔلُوٓاْ أَهْلَ ٱلذِّكْرِ...﴾

Part 4

The Major Signs - Verses 16-18

إِذۡ يَغۡشَى ٱلسِّدۡرَةَ مَا يَغۡشَىٰ ﴿١٦﴾ مَا زَاغَ ٱلۡبَصَرُ وَمَا طَغَىٰ ﴿١٧﴾ لَقَدۡ
رَأَىٰ مِنۡ ءَايَٰتِ رَبِّهِ ٱلۡكُبۡرَىٰٓ ﴿١٨﴾

16. When there covered the Lotus Tree that which covered it.

17. The sight (of the Prophet) did not waver, nor did it transgress (its limit).

18. Indeed he saw some of the greatest signs of his Lord.

Thinking Points

In the first verse of Sūrah al-Isrāʾ (17) we read that Allah ﷻ took His Prophet ﷺ on a Night Journey so that He could show him some of His signs: 'So that We may show him (Muḥammad) from Our signs;' and in this chapter under review we read that Allah ﷻ showed the Prophet ﷺ some of His signs: 'Indeed he saw some of the greatest signs of his Lord.'

It must be kept in mind that the Noble Prophet ﷺ was immaculate *(maʿṣūm)* in every way, some of which include the following:

1. His thoughts and actions - 'Your companion has not gone astray.'[35]

---

[35] Quran, Sūrah al-Najm (53), verse 2.

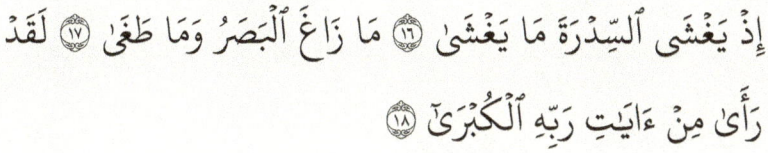

2. His speech - 'Nor does he speak out of his own desire.'[36]
3. His knowledge - 'Taught to him by the Extremely Powerful.'[37]
4. His spiritual heart - 'The heart did not lie about what it saw.'[38]
5. His eyesight - 'The sight did not waver, nor did it exceed.'[39]

Take Away Messages

1. The right of the power of sight is that it must not be used to look at that which is forbidden (according to the laws of Allah ﷻ), nor should it be used to transgress the limits (of what it can look at).
2. The only time that the eyes will have the ability to witness the great signs of the Divine are when they are [at the spiritual level of] being eyes which can see and perceive the actual reality of things.
3. The signs of the Divine are so vast that even the best creation (the Prophet of Islam ﷺ) is only able to see <u>some</u> of them.

---

[36] Quran, Sūrah al-Najm (53), verse 3.

[37] Ibid., verse 5.

[38] Ibid., verse 11.

[39] Ibid., verse 17.

Part 5

The Idols - Verses 19-22

أَفَرَءَيْتُمُ ٱللَّٰتَ وَٱلْعُزَّىٰ ﴿١٩﴾ وَمَنَوٰةَ ٱلثَّالِثَةَ ٱلْأُخْرَىٰٓ ﴿٢٠﴾ أَلَكُمُ ٱلذَّكَرُ
وَلَهُ ٱلْأُنثَىٰ ﴿٢١﴾ تِلْكَ إِذًا قِسْمَةٌ ضِيزَىٰٓ ﴿٢٢﴾

19. Have you considered al-Lāt and al-ʿUzza?

20. And Manāt, the third one, the other?

21. Is the male for you, and for Him the female?

22. That is an unjust distribution.

Thinking Points

What comparison can ever be drawn between Allah ﷻ - the One who is so Powerful that He is able to take a human being to the pinnacles of the heavens and show him some of His greatest signs - and stone idols who have absolutely no powers whatsoever!?

It should be noted that in the Quran, there are nine different idols whose names have been mentioned:

In this chapter of the Quran (Sūrah al-Najm), three of them are named:

1. *Lāt*
2. *ʿUzza*
3. *Manāt*

In another verse[40] there is one mentioned:

4. *Baʿl*

In another verse of the Quran[41] the names of the other five idols have been given:

1. *Wudda*
2. *Suwāʿ*
3. *Yaghūth*
4. *Yaʿūq*
5. *Nasra*

Take Away Messages

1. When we look [at things around us] it must be done for a purpose.
2. Those who are propagators and educators of the faith must be aware of the things [in society] which are causing people to deviate and go astray.
3. Sometimes it is necessary to acquaint the people in society with the various ways and means as well as those individuals that are the causes of deviancy and misguidedness. There are times when we must expose and condemn them so that other people can learn from such examples, keep away from them, and be guided to the path of salvation.

---

[40] Quran, Sūrah al-Ṣāffāt (37), verse 125:

﴿أَتَدْعُونَ بَعْلًا وَتَذَرُونَ أَحْسَنَ ٱلْخَٰلِقِينَ ١٢٥﴾

[41] Ibid., Sūrah Nūḥ (71), verse 23:

﴿وَقَالُوا۟ لَا تَذَرُنَّ ءَالِهَتَكُمْ وَلَا تَذَرُنَّ وَدًّا وَلَا سُوَاعًا وَلَا يَغُوثَ وَيَعُوقَ وَنَسْرًا ٢٣﴾

4. When it comes to reformation, one must start with going to the sources; for example, when it comes to destroying false idols, one must begin by attacking and destroying the biggest of them primarily - just as Allah ﷻ says in the Quran: 'So then fight (against) the leaders of disbelief.'[42]
5. Whatever a person does not like for oneself, one must also detest that for others - as the Quran clearly states in this passage where Allah ﷻ says: 'Is the male for you and for Him the female!?' Since the polytheists of that era despised having daughters, why did they then take the liberty to call the angels as the daughters of Allah ﷻ?
6. When it comes to guidance, one should make use of asking questions – to the right people - to get the point across.

[42] Quran, Sūrah al-Tawbah (9), verse 12:

﴿وَإِن نَّكَثُوٓاْ أَيۡمَٰنَهُم مِّنۢ بَعۡدِ عَهۡدِهِمۡ وَطَعَنُواْ فِي دِينِكُمۡ فَقَٰتِلُوٓاْ أَئِمَّةَ ٱلۡكُفۡرِ إِنَّهُمۡ لَآ أَيۡمَٰنَ لَهُمۡ لَعَلَّهُمۡ يَنتَهُونَ ١٢﴾

Part 6

Falsehood - Verse 23

إِنْ هِيَ إِلَّآ أَسْمَآءٌ سَمَّيْتُمُوهَآ أَنتُمْ وَءَابَآؤُكُم مَّآ أَنزَلَ
ٱللَّهُ بِهَا مِن سُلْطَٰنٍ ۚ إِن يَتَّبِعُونَ إِلَّا ٱلظَّنَّ وَمَا تَهْوَى ٱلْأَنفُسُ ۖ
وَلَقَدْ جَآءَهُم مِّن رَّبِّهِمُ ٱلْهُدَىٰٓ ﴿٢٣﴾

23. These are nothing but names which you have devised - you and your ancestors - for which Allah sent down no authority. They follow nothing but assumptions, and what the ego desires, even though guidance has come to them from their Lord.

Thinking Points

The word '*sulṭān*' meaning 'authority,' when used in the Quran, is proof and evidence which is the source of domination.

The idolaters considered each one of their idols to be a manifestation of a universal action: one was the expression of power, one was for knowledge, one for love, one for anger, etc... but in the face of such beliefs, the Quran says: "Go ahead and fill your mouths with these names and titles, however realize that truly they have no authenticity to them, and these names have no actual reality in the real world."

Take Away Messages

1. We must not pay any attention to every slogan, title, and epithet that is thrown around.
2. A person's ancestors are those who shape the culture for the proceeding generations.
3. It is forbidden to blindly imitate one's forefathers.
4. Polytheism has its roots and originates from the imagination and blind devotion to the past and has no logical backing to it.
5. Beliefs must be based on proofs, as speculation and blind imitation of others is not sufficient.
6. Guidance comes from Allah ﷻ, while misguidance stems from one's lower desires.
7. Following the lower desires has been condemned.
8. Allah ﷻ completed the argument over everyone, and once the revelation reaches humanity, they have no further excuses (to disbelieve in Allah ﷻ).
9. Guidance and direction come from Allah ﷻ.
10. Anytime a person condemns the erroneous ways (of others), one must at the same time show the right path to follow.
11. The way of knowledge and revelation is the way of the truth, as the Quran says: 'The guidance has come to them from their Lord.' However, personal tastes - 'all of you,' and one's forefathers - 'your fathers,' and the paths of presumption and conjecture - 'nothing other than conjecture,' and the path of one's lower, base desires - '...and the low desires which (their) souls incline to...' are all invalid.

Part 7

The Authority - Verses 24-26

أَمْ لِلْإِنسَٰنِ مَا تَمَنَّىٰ ﴿٢٤﴾ فَلِلَّهِ ٱلْءَاخِرَةُ وَٱلْأُولَىٰ ﴿٢٥﴾ وَكَم مِّن مَّلَكٍ فِي
ٱلسَّمَٰوَٰتِ لَا تُغْنِي شَفَٰعَتُهُمْ شَيْـًٔا إِلَّا مِنۢ بَعْدِ أَن يَأْذَنَ ٱللَّهُ لِمَن
يَشَآءُ وَيَرْضَىٰٓ ﴿٢٦﴾

24. Or is the human being to have whatever one desires?

25. To Allah belongs the last (hereafter) and the first (this life).

26. And how many an angel is there in the heavens whose intercession avails nothing, except after Allah gives permission to whomsoever He wills, and approves?

Thinking Points

The meaning of the word '*tamannā*' is 'hopes and desires' - whether these be things which are possible to attain, or impossible to reach, and regardless of whether they are logical or illogical;[43] however the word '*rajā*' is used in those instances for 'hopes which are attainable;' the word '*ṭamāʿa*' is used for 'wishes whose attainment is close at hand;' and the word '*amal*' is used in those instances in which it is 'difficult to attain that longing.'[44]

---

[43] *Al-Mufradāt.*

[44] *Furūq al-Lughāt.*

To reform an individual, Islam seeks to modify the thinking process of the person, so to ensure that a person does not run around aimlessly seeking greatness and power for oneself, Allah ﷻ declares: "Indeed all greatness belongs solely to Allah;"[45] and "Indeed all power belongs solely to Allah."[46]

In this verse under review Allah ﷻ tells us that: "The world to come and this world all belong exclusively to Allah, so why then do you pin your hopes on other than Him!?"

The universe is in motion through His will - not through our desire, and in this regards, Imam ʿAlī ؑ has been quoted as saying: "I came to know Allah, the Glorified, through the breaking of determinations, resolving of the problems, and breaching the decisions."[47]

In saying this, the Imam ؑ wants us to understand that Allah ﷻ alone controls the world and everything that is within it, and it is not our longings or inclinations which play any role in this.

Imam al-Ṣādiq ؑ has been quoted as saying that: "Neither can the angels, nor the Prophet save you from the wrath of Allah, and if anyone is seeking intercession *(shafāʿat)*, then let them look for it in the Pleasure of Allah."[48]

---

[45] Quran, Sūrah al-Nisāʾ (4), verse 139:

﴿...فَإِنَّ ٱلْعِزَّةَ لِلَّهِ جَمِيعًا ﴿١٣٩﴾﴾

[46] Ibid., Sūrah al-Baqarah (2), verse 165:

﴿...إِنَّ الْقُوَّةَ لِلَّهِ جَمِيعاً...﴾

[47] *Nahj al-Balāgha*, Short Saying 250:
عَرَفْتُ اللّٰهَ سُبْحَانَهُ بِفَسْخِ الْعَزَائِمِ وَحَلِّ الْعُقُودِ

[48] *Biḥār al-Anwār*, Vol. 8, Pg. 53.

When it comes to intercession, a question may come up: Is intercession not some sort of favouritism?

The answer to this question is: Not at all, and the reasons below explain why:

1. A person who is wanting to have someone intercede for them (with Allah ﷻ) will attempt to be worthy of being interceded for through their thoughts and actions; thus, this goes against favouritism. Therefore, intercession has certain rules and criteria before it can be realized.
2. When it comes to intercession, the rights of other people are not stripped away from anyone; however, in favouritism, the rights of others are transgressed.
3. The intercessor expects nothing back from the person whom one is interceding for; however, when it comes to favouritism, the one who steps in and engages in such political games always expects something back in return for one's favour.
4. The goal of an intercessor is to ensure salvation in the world to come for the one whom they are interceding for; however, the goal of favouritism is to provide material gains in this world.
5. Intercession is a means of nurturing and spiritual growth in this world because the person who is seeking to benefit from the intercession of someone will try to establish a strong spiritual connection with the close friends of Allah ﷻ *(awliyāʾ)* from whom one is seeking intercession.

The meaning of 'whomever He permits' in verse 26 of this chapter as it relates to the theme of intercession can be understood in two different ways:

1. Whomsoever Allah ﷻ wishes, He will grant them the power to intercede for other people.

2. Whomsoever Allah ﷻ desires, He will grant them the right to have others intercede for them.

At this point, another question comes up which is: Would the fact that one person can intercede for another person in the court of Allah ﷻ not lead to people being encouraged to sin more?

The answer to this question is that: This can never be the case! First off, it is not clear as to who will be allowed to intercede for others; and secondly, like the example of someone who has been poisoned - just because a medication is available to save such an individual, does this mean that we should now encourage people to swallow poison? Of course not!

A Review of the Concept of Aspirations in the Quran and *Aḥādīth*

The Significance of Having "Aspirations"

Aspiring in life is a factor which leads to change and progress. The Noble Prophet ﷺ has been quoted as saying: "Had there not been aspirations in the lives of people, no mother would ever breastfeed her child, and no farmer would ever plant one's crops."[49]

Prophet 'Isā ﷺ once saw an old man holding a shovel, plowing the ground [to plant something] and he said: "O Allah! Take away the desire of aspiration from this old man." Instantaneously he saw the old man throw his shovel aside and go to sleep. After a period, Prophet 'Isā ﷺ once again asked Allah to return aspirations to that

---

[49] *Biḥār al-Anwār*, Vol. 77, Pg. 137:

لَوْ لاَ الأَمَلُ مَا رَضِعَتْ وَالِدَةٌ وَلَدِهَا وَلاَ غَرَسَ غَارِسٌ شَجَرَهَا

old man and he saw the man get up and start to work on his fields again.⁵⁰

Restraining Our Aspirations

Our aspirations must be controlled by the foundational pillars of facilities, abilities, conditions, and spiritual capacities - and if these are not in place then such aspirations will become nothing more than foolish dreams.

In this regard, Imam ʿAlī has said: "My greatest concern for you is following your base desires and having long drawn out aspirations [that cannot be attained]."⁵¹

Negative Aspirations

There are some types of aspirations which have been criticized and forbidden in the noble Quran, such as those people who wish that they had vast amounts of wealth like what Qārūn possessed: "O would that we had the like of what Qārūn was given."⁵²

Or like in another verse, the aspiration that some people have where they want unwarranted praise heaped upon them: "And love that they should be praised for what they did not do."⁵³

Or there is an aspiration which some people have that they want to be looked at as being greater than others in society: "(As

---

⁵⁰ *Biḥār al-Anwār*, Vol. 14, Pg. 329.

⁵¹ *Nahj al-Balāgha*, Sermon 28.

⁵² Quran, Sūrah al-Qaṣaṣ (28), verse 79:

﴾...يَا لَيْتَ لَنَا مِثْلَ مَا أُوتِيَ قَارُونَ...﴿

⁵³ Ibid., Sūrah Āle ʿImrān (3), verse 188:

﴾...يُحِبُّونَ أَنْ يُحْمَدُوا بِمَا لَمْ يَفْعَلُوا...﴿

for) that future abode (in the hereafter), We assign it to those who have no desire to exalt themselves in the earth, nor make mischief; and the (best) outcome is for those who guard (against evil)."[54]

Many times, in the Quran, we see that Allah ﷻ uses the below statements: "So let not their property or their children impress you."[55] And "Do not strain your eyes towards that which We have given certain classes of them to enjoy."[56]

By doing this, Allah ﷻ is seeking to warn the believers that they should not look at the wealth which others have with negative aspirations, otherwise they may take a root in themselves.

Irresolvable Aspirations

On the Day of Judgement, one of the sentences which the guilty people will repeatedly say is 'يَا لَيْتَنِي' - 'O, if only!' or 'O, I wish...'

However, what benefit is there at that time when it will be too late to do anything! The culpable will make statements such as: "O, if only I were dust!"[57]

---

[54] Quran, Sūrah al-Qaṣaṣ (28), verse 83:

﴿تِلْكَ ٱلدَّارُ ٱلْـَٔاخِرَةُ نَجْعَلُهَا لِلَّذِينَ لَا يُرِيدُونَ عُلُوًّا فِى ٱلْأَرْضِ وَلَا فَسَادًا ۚ وَٱلْعَـٰقِبَةُ لِلْمُتَّقِينَ ﴿٨٣﴾﴾

[55] Ibid., Sūrah al-Tawbah (9), verses 55 and 85 (with a slight variation in the wording):

﴿فَلَا تُعْجِبْكَ أَمْوَالُهُمْ وَلَا أَوْلَادُهُمْ...﴾

[56] Ibid., Sūrah al-Ḥijr (15), verse 88; Sūrah Ṭāhā (20), verse 131 (with a slight variation in the wording):

﴿لَا تَمُدَّنَّ عَيْنَيْكَ إِلَىٰ مَا مَتَّعْنَا بِهِ أَزْوَاجًا مِنْهُمْ...﴾

[57] Ibid., Sūrah al-Naba' (78), verse 40:

﴿...يَا لَيْتَنِي كُنْتُ تُرَابًا﴾

Dirt has the power to take a seed that is planted within it and give back a plant; it also has the power to take dirty water and in return give back pure, potable water. However, there are some people whose entire life is full of corruption - and thus they give back nothing positive to society, making them even worse than dirt.

We see many examples of this 'O, if only' in the Quran, some of which include the following: "O, if only I had taken a path with the Messenger."[58] "O, I wish my book had never been given to me."[59] "They will say: O, I wish I had sent (ahead some good) for my life!"[60] "O, if only we could be sent back (to life on earth) and not reject the signs of our Lord."[61]

Take Away Messages

1. Do not leave the way of Allah ﷻ with the hopes of the intercession of others, as with this thought, a person will not be able to achieve either one - neither intercession, nor closeness to Allah ﷻ.

---

[58] Quran, Sūrah al-Furqān (25), verse 27:

﴿...يَقُولُ يَٰلَيۡتَنِي ٱتَّخَذۡتُ مَعَ ٱلرَّسُولِ سَبِيلٗا ٢٧﴾

[59] Ibid., Sūrah al-Ḥāqqah (69), verse 25:

﴿...فَيَقُولُ يَٰلَيۡتَنِي لَمۡ أُوتَ كِتَٰبِيَهۡ ٢٥﴾

[60] Ibid., Sūrah al-Fajr (89), verse 24:

﴿يَقُولُ يَٰلَيۡتَنِي قَدَّمۡتُ لِحَيَاتِي ٢٤﴾

[61] Ibid., Sūrah al-Anʿām (6), verse 27:

﴿...يَا لَيْتَنَا نُرَدُّ وَ لاَ نُكَذِّبَ بِآيَاتِ رَبِّنَا...﴾

2. Both the abandonment of the Divine guidance - 'The guidance from their Lord,' and running after unattainable desires have been condemned in the faith.
3. The absolute authority in the hereafter and this world belong solely to Allah ﷻ; thus, we must never go in search of either of these from other than Him.
4. Other than Allah ﷻ, whoever and whatever else that exists is transient and short-lived.
5. The principle of this world is that it is founded on the Omnipotence of Allah ﷻ - whether our wishes are compatible with it.
6. The clearest manifestation of the Ownership of Allah ﷻ will be displayed on the Day of Resurrection, and this can be seen in the verse of the Quran in which Allah ﷻ says 'the next life and this world' as He mentions the 'next life' before mentioning 'this world.'
7. Even the closest of angels have no power of intercession without the permission of Allah ﷻ - let alone the idols!
8. Since the next world and this world exclusively belong to Allah ﷻ and Him alone, His pleasure and consent are required for any kind of intercession to take shape.
9. Not every person has the right to intercede, nor does every individual who acted unjustly have the right to receive intercession. Rather, intercession is only for those people whom Allah ﷻ permits, and there is no doubt that the will of Allah ﷻ is based on wisdom and in accordance with certain principles and rules.

Part 8

No Substitutes - Verses 27-28

إِنَّ ٱلَّذِينَ لَا يُؤْمِنُونَ بِٱلْـَٔاخِرَةِ لَيُسَمُّونَ ٱلْمَلَـٰٓئِكَةَ تَسْمِيَةَ ٱلْأُنثَىٰ ﴿٢٧﴾
وَمَا لَهُم بِهِۦ مِنْ عِلْمٍ ۖ إِن يَتَّبِعُونَ إِلَّا ٱلظَّنَّ ۖ وَإِنَّ ٱلظَّنَّ لَا يُغْنِى مِنَ
ٱلْحَقِّ شَيْـًٔا ﴿٢٨﴾

27. Those who do not believe in the hereafter give the angels the names of females.

28. And they have no knowledge of that, they only follow assumptions, and assumptions are no substitute for the truth.

Thinking Points

Anything that is based on true and accurate knowledge will always be regarded as being correct, and every truth is in accordance with true and accurate knowledge - they are both the same. Although the Quran could have said: 'Having assumptions about something should not stop a person from seeking real knowledge about that thing,' it says it in a different way that: 'Having assumptions about something should not stop a person from seeking the truth about that thing' - since the truth (*al-ḥaqq*) and true knowledge (*al-'ilm*) are one and the same.

Naming the angels with the names of females was based on unfounded beliefs, as they (the Arabs during the Era of Ignorance - *Jāhiliyyah*) considered the angels to be the daughters of Allah ﷻ.

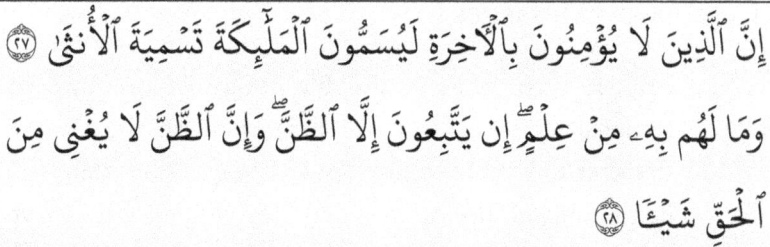

Those individuals who paint portraits of the angels in the form of females are basing their works on the Period of Ignorance - even if they unknowingly engage in this.

Take Away Messages

1. Anyone who, while in this life, feels that they will be responsible in the court of judgement on the Day of Resurrection, will not just say anything; rather they will be cautious of their speech, and they will not just believe in any speculation which comes their way.
2. Do not consider the process of giving someone a name as being trivial. Those who give bad names (or nicknames) to others have been rebuked in Islam.
3. Someone who has no knowledge about something must remain silent regarding that.
4. Wherever knowledge is lacking, there will be a vacuum for speculation to take over.
5. When it comes to the religious belief system, having speculation is not enough - one must have proper knowledge.

Part 9

The Paths - Verses 29-30

فَأَعۡرِضۡ عَن مَّن تَوَلَّىٰ عَن ذِكۡرِنَا وَلَمۡ يُرِدۡ إِلَّا ٱلۡحَيَوٰةَ ٱلدُّنۡيَا ۝٢٩
ذَٰلِكَ مَبۡلَغُهُم مِّنَ ٱلۡعِلۡمِۚ إِنَّ رَبَّكَ هُوَ أَعۡلَمُ بِمَن ضَلَّ عَن سَبِيلِهِۦ
وَهُوَ أَعۡلَمُ بِمَنِ ٱهۡتَدَىٰ ۝٣٠

29. So avoid the one who has turned away from Our remembrance, and desires nothing but the present life.

30. That is the extent of their knowledge. Your Lord knows best who has strayed from His path, and He knows best who has accepted guidance.

Thinking Points

Within the Quran, the command 'to avoid' or 'turn away from' has been mentioned on several occasions, some of which including the following:

1. The disbelievers: Therefore, turn away from them...[62]
2. The polytheists: ...And withdraw from the polytheists.[63]

---

[62] Quran, Sūrah al-Sajdah (32), verse 30:

﴿فَأَعۡرِضۡ عَنۡهُمۡ...﴾

[63] Ibid., Sūrah al-Anʿām (6), verse 106:

﴿...وَأَعۡرِضۡ عَنِ ٱلۡمُشۡرِكِينَ ۝١٠٦﴾

3. The hypocrites: They are the enemy, therefore beware of them...[64]
4. The ignorant ones: ...And turn aside from the ignorant.[65]
5. Those who run away from the war front: ...So do turn aside from them.[66]
6. Those who pretend to seek guidance from the Divine revelations, however, do so only to ridicule them: ...Withdraw from them...[67]

In many verses of the Noble Quran, the visage and temporary nature of life in this transient world has been shown to us, such as in the following passages:

1. This transient world is trivial and irrelevant: ...The provision of this world is short.[68]

---

[64] Quran, Sūrah al-Munāfiqūn (63), verse 4:

﴿هُمُ الْعَدُوُّ فَاحْذَرْهُمْ...﴾

[65] Ibid., Sūrah al-Aʿrāf (7), verse 199:

﴿...وَأَعْرِضْ عَنِ ٱلْجَٰهِلِينَ ١٩٩﴾

[66] Ibid., Sūrah al-Tawbah (9), verse 95:

﴿...فَأَعْرِضُوا عَنْهُمْ...﴾

[67] Ibid., Sūrah al-Anʿām (6), verse 68:

﴿...فَأَعْرِضْ عَنْهُمْ...﴾

[68] Ibid., Sūrah al-Nisāʾ (4), verse 77:

﴿...مَتَاعُ الدُّنْيَا قَلِيلٌ...﴾

2. This transient world will perish, and it is merely a place to pass through, not to stay: "What is with you (of this transient world) will end (pass away)."[69]
3. An attachment to this transient world is nothing more than an exercise in vain and futile activity: "And the life of this world is nothing but amusement and play."[70]
4. This transient world is a means of distraction: "And this world's life is nothing but a means of deception."[71]
5. An attachment to this transient world will prevent a person from seeking the world to come: "Are you satisfied with the life of this world instead of the hereafter?"[72]
6. This transient world is a place of enchantment: "O, if only we had the like of what was given to Qārūn."[73]

In the Quran, there are five characteristics of this transient world which have been mentioned, and these fit with the five stages of the life of a human being. In this verse, a portion of it reads: "Know

---

69 Quran, Sūrah al-Naḥl (16), verse 96:

﴿مَا عِنْدَكُمْ يَنْفَدُ...﴾

70 Ibid., Sūrah al-ʿAnkabūt (29), verse 64:

﴿وَمَا هٰذِهِ الْحَيَاةُ الدُّنْيَا إِلاَّ لَهْوٌ وَ لَعِبٌ...﴾

71 Ibid., Sūrah al-Ḥadīd (57), verse 20:

﴿...وَمَا ٱلْحَيَوٰةُ ٱلدُّنْيَآ إِلَّا مَتَٰعُ ٱلْغُرُورِ ۝٢٠﴾

72 Ibid., Sūrah al-Tawbah (9), verse 38:

﴿...أَرَضِيتُمْ بِالْحَيَاةِ الدُّنْيَا مِنَ الآخِرَةِ...﴾

73 Ibid., Sūrah al-Qaṣaṣ (28), verse 79:

﴿...يَا لَيْتَ لَنَا مِثْلَ مَا أُوتِيَ قَارُونَ...﴾

that the life of this world is only amusement and play, and temporary attraction and boasting among yourselves, and competition in the increase of wealth and children."[74]

These stages are as follows:

1. Amusement - Infancy.
2. Play - Child.
3. Temporary attraction - Young adult.
4. Boasting amongst yourselves - Middle aged.
5. Rivalry in the multiplication of wealth and children - Old age.

Indeed, this transient world is just a means to the result, not a final goal; like we read in a supplication which has been recommended to recite in the month of Shaʿbān: "And do not make this transient world our greatest concern."[75]

Take Away Messages

1. Do not be discouraged when dealing with those who are centered on this transient world and are not focused on Allah ﷻ.
2. It is better to turn away from those who reject the religion of Allah ﷻ and refuse to hear His Name and commands. We should note that in Islam, the boycott of opponents and enemies is permissible.

---

[74] Quran, Sūrah al-Ḥadīd (57), verse 20:

﴿اعْلَمُوا أَنَّمَا الْحَيَاةُ الدُّنْيَا لَعِبٌ وَلَهْوٌ وَزِينَةٌ وَتَفَاخُرٌ بَيْنَكُمْ وَتَكَاثُرٌ فِي الْأَمْوَالِ وَالْأَوْلَادِ...﴾

[75] *Mafātīḥ al-Jinān*:

وَلاَ تَجْعَلِ الدُّنْيَا أَكْبَرَ هَمِّنَا...

3. Distancing ourselves from the enemies of Islam *(al-tabarrī)* is one of the principles of faith.
4. Do not waste time and opportunities in the propagation of religion in areas where you know there will be no benefit.
5. Sometimes counter-acting is necessary. Those who turn away from Allah ﷻ should likewise also be turned away from and ignored (just as they ignore Allah ﷻ).
6. Materialism and turning away from Allah ﷻ are interconnected.
7. Although struggling and working hard in the life of this world and having a natural attraction to the life here is something which has been looked at in a favourable light in Islam, at the same time, we have been strongly advised to limit our thoughts and actions to merely the temporal pleasures of the life of this world.
8. Materialism is a sign of a low level of understanding and knowledge.
9. Those who think about nothing other than the life of this transient world are misled.
10. Belief in the Knowledge of Allah ﷻ and supervision of the actions when it comes to the life of a human being is a cause of comfort and ease for a believer.
11. Turning away from Allah ﷻ and making this transient world the focal point of one's life is a clear indication of deviation.
12. Allah ﷻ knows the deeds and intentions of each one of His servants.

Part 10

Infinite Justice - Verse 31

وَلِلَّهِ مَا فِي ٱلسَّمَٰوَٰتِ وَمَا فِي ٱلْأَرْضِ لِيَجْزِيَ ٱلَّذِينَ أَسَٰٓـُٔواْ بِمَا عَمِلُواْ
وَيَجْزِيَ ٱلَّذِينَ أَحْسَنُواْ بِٱلْحُسْنَى ٣١

31. To Allah belongs whatever is in the heavens and whatever is on earth. He will repay those who do evil according to their deeds, and recompense those who do good with the best.

Thinking Points

In the previous verse we read that there are some people who reject the remembrance of Allah ﷻ and other than this temporal, material world, they think about nothing else.

This verse continues that theme and seeks to tell us that: "Turning away from the One" - from whom everything emanates and the One in whose hands are the rewards and punishments - is to be in a state of complete denial. If you are seeking the goodness of this transient world, then you must not turn away from Him, as He owns both the next world and this current, temporary world.

The vast expanse of the skies is much greater than that of the earth, and it is for this reason that the Quran starts off by mentioning 'the skies' and then it mentions 'the earth.'

Take Away Messages

1. For punishments and rewards to be meted out fairly, the one who is handing them out needs to be knowledgeable and fully capable.
2. The entire system of creation has been put into place for a reason.
3. The rewards of the Divine are much greater than the good deeds of a human being, however the punishments from Allah ﷻ are NOT more than the bad actions of an individual. This is all due to the Mercy of Allah ﷻ.
4. The eventual outcome of a human being is in one's own hands (due to their actions in this world).

Part 11

Vast Forgiveness - Verse 32

ٱلَّذِينَ يَجۡتَنِبُونَ كَبَٰٓئِرَ ٱلۡإِثۡمِ وَٱلۡفَوَٰحِشَ إِلَّا ٱللَّمَمَۚ إِنَّ رَبَّكَ وَٰسِعُ
ٱلۡمَغۡفِرَةِۚ هُوَ أَعۡلَمُ بِكُمۡ إِذۡ أَنشَأَكُم مِّنَ ٱلۡأَرۡضِ وَإِذۡ أَنتُمۡ أَجِنَّةٞ فِي
بُطُونِ أُمَّهَٰتِكُمۡۖ فَلَا تُزَكُّوٓاْ أَنفُسَكُمۡۖ هُوَ أَعۡلَمُ بِمَنِ ٱتَّقَىٰٓ ٣٢

32. Those who avoid gross sins and indecencies - except for minor lapses - your Lord is of Vast Forgiveness. He knows you well, ever since He created you from the earth, and ever since you were embryos in your mothers' wombs. So do not acclaim your own virtue; He is fully Aware of the righteous ones.

Thinking Points

The word '*fawāḥish*' is the plural of '*fāḥishah*' and it is used when speaking about 'any type of indecent sin such as adultery or fornication.'

Regarding the word '*lamama*' within the traditions,[76] in the books of Arabic grammar and commentaries of the Quran, there are various meanings that have been mentioned, some of which include the following:

1. A sin that is performed unintentionally, and which a person is not persistent in performing.

---

[76] *Al-Kāfī*, Vol. 2, Pg. 422.

2. A sin which a person decided to perform, however never actually followed through with the action.
3. A sin which was performed, however immediately afterwards, the person sought forgiveness for doing it, and turned back to Allah ﷻ in repentance.
4. A sin for which no specific punishment has been mentioned (in the Islamic sources).
5. A sin for which no specific legal punishment (in this world) has been mentioned.

The issue of a sin being 'big' or 'small' has been spoken about numerous times in the Quran;[77] and the fact that every action of a human being is being recorded has also been mentioned in the Quran, as Allah ﷻ says: 'And every small and big (action) is written down.'[78]

How a person's file of actions will be shown on the Day of Judgement has also been noted in the Quran where Allah ﷻ says: 'And We will bring forth to them on the Day of Resurrection a book which one will find wide open;'[79] and at that time, a loud cry

---

77 Quran, Sūrah al-Nisā' (4), verse 31; Sūrah al-Kahf (18), verse 49; Sūrah al-Shūra' (42), verse 37; and Sūrah al-Qamar (54), verse 53:

﴿إِن تَجْتَنِبُوا۟ كَبَآئِرَ مَا تُنْهَوْنَ عَنْهُ نُكَفِّرْ عَنكُمْ سَيِّـَٔاتِكُمْ وَنُدْخِلْكُم مُّدْخَلًا كَرِيمًا ٣١﴾

78 Ibid., Sūrah al-Qamar (54), verse 53:

﴿وَكُلُّ صَغِيرٍ وَكَبِيرٍ مُّسْتَطَرٌ ٥٣﴾

79 Ibid., Sūrah al-Isrā' (17), verse 13:

﴿وَكُلَّ إِنسَٰنٍ أَلْزَمْنَٰهُ طَٰٓئِرَهُۥ فِى عُنُقِهِۦ ۖ وَنُخْرِجُ لَهُۥ يَوْمَ ٱلْقِيَٰمَةِ كِتَٰبًا يَلْقَىٰهُ مَنشُورًا ١٣﴾

will be heard proclaiming: 'O, woe to us! What is this book that leaves nothing small or great, except that it has enumerated it?'[80]

When it comes to the 'major sins' Imam al-Riḍā has listed them as being the following actions:

1. Killing an innocent person.
2. Illicit sexual relationships (outside of the bounds of marriage).
3. Theft.
4. Consuming intoxicants.
5. Displeasing one's parents which results in them disowning their child.
6. Fleeing from the war front.
7. Misappropriating the property of an orphan.
8. Eating the meat of an animal which has died on its own.
9. Consuming blood.
10. Eating anything which comes from a pig.
11. Consuming anything which has not been slaughtered according to the rules of Islam.
12. Engaging in interest-bearing transactions.
13. Taking bribes.
14. Gambling.
15. Not being truthful and fair in business dealings.
16. Making false accusations of sexual impropriety against chaste women (or people in general).
17. Homosexuality.
18. Bearing false witness.

---

[80] Quran, Sūrah al-Kahf (18), verse 49:

﴿وَوُضِعَ ٱلْكِتَٰبُ فَتَرَى ٱلْمُجْرِمِينَ مُشْفِقِينَ مِمَّا فِيهِ وَيَقُولُونَ يَٰوَيْلَتَنَا مَالِ هَٰذَا ٱلْكِتَٰبِ لَا يُغَادِرُ صَغِيرَةً وَلَا كَبِيرَةً إِلَّآ أَحْصَىٰهَا ۚ وَوَجَدُوا۟ مَا عَمِلُوا۟ حَاضِرًا ۗ وَلَا يَظْلِمُ رَبُّكَ أَحَدًا ﴿٤٩﴾﴾

19. Having despair in the Mercy of Allah ﷻ.
20. Feeling immune from the Divine retribution.
21. Losing complete hope in the Mercy of Allah ﷻ.
22. Helping or relying upon the oppressors.
23. Making a false oath.
24. Not giving others their rights.
25. Lying.
26. Being arrogant.
27. Extravagance or miserliness (in any area of life).
28. Being treacherous.
29. Being indifferent in terms of the performance of *ḥajj* (when it has become an obligation upon an individual).
30. Having enmity for the close friends *(awliyāʾ)* of Allah ﷻ.
31. Busying oneself with things that fall into the category of *lahw* and *laʿib* - things such as the forbidden types of music, entertainment, etc.
32. The continuous performance of sins.[81]

Regarding the sentence from this verse where Allah ﷻ says: 'so do not acclaim your own virtue,' Imam al-Bāqir (ʿa) has been quoted as saying that: "Do not be proud due to your prayers *(ṣalāt)*, charity *(zakāt)*, fasting *(ṣawm)*, and other actions of worship, as Allah best knows the people who are truly God-consciousness (have *taqwā*)."[82]

It was once asked of Imam al-Ṣādiq (ʿa): "Is it permissible for a person to compliment and praise oneself?" The Imam (ʿa) replied: "If there is some necessity which requires a person to do this, then it is not a problem." The Imam (ʿa) then added: "Have you not heard that when [Prophet] Yūsuf went to the Governor of Egypt, he

[81] *Tafsīr Nūr al-Thaqalayn.*

[82] *Tafsīr Kanz al-Daqāʾiq.*

began to praise himself and said: 'Place me (in authority) over the treasures of the land, surely I am a good keeper, knowing well.'"[83]

Once, Imam ʿAlī overheard a group of people talking and boasting about themselves saying: "Yesterday, I was busy in prayers for the entire night until the morning prayers, and in addition, I fasted yesterday too." To this, Imam ʿAlī said to them: "Yesterday, I slept the entire night, and I did not fast." By saying this, he was showing us that sometimes in order to put an end to pride and arrogance of others, such words must be uttered (by the leaders of the faith).

Imam Jaʿfar al-Ṣādiq said that: "Once, a Jewish man came to the Prophet and stood in front of him, staring at him. The Prophet asked: 'O Jew! What do you want?'

The Jewish man replied: 'Are you more virtuous, or Mūsā, the son of ʿImrān - the Prophet whom Allah spoke to, the one who was given the Tawrāt and the staff, for whom the sea was split, and who was shaded by the cloud?'

In response, the Prophet replied: 'It is disliked for a servant [of Allah] to praise oneself, but I will say that: When Ādam made the mistake, he repented by saying: 'O Allah! I ask You, by the right of Muḥammad and the family of Muḥammad, to forgive me,' then Allah pardoned him for his actions. When Nūḥ boarded the Ark and feared drowning, he said: 'O Allah! I ask You, by the right of Muḥammad and the family of Muḥammad, to save me from drowning,' so Allah saved him from that. When Ibrāhīm was thrown into the fire, he said: 'O Allah! I ask You, by the right of Muḥammad and the family of Muḥammad, to deliver me from this,'

---

[83] Quran, Sūrah Yūsuf (12), verse 55:

﴿قَالَ ٱجْعَلْنِى عَلَىٰ خَزَآئِنِ ٱلْأَرْضِ إِنِّى حَفِيظٌ عَلِيمٌ۝﴾

so Allah made it [the fire] cool and peaceful. When Mūsā (عليه السلام) cast his staff and felt fear in himself, he said: 'O Allah! I ask You, by the right of Muḥammad and the family of Muḥammad, to keep me safe from this,' thus Allah said: 'Fear not. Surely, it is you who is superior.' (Sūrah Ṭāhā (20), verse 68)

O Jew! [Even] if Mūsā were to meet me and disbelieve in me and my Prophethood, then his faith would not avail him at all, nor would his Prophethood be of any benefit for him. O Jew! From my progeny is the Mahdī. When he appears, 'Isā, the son of Maryam, will descend to support him, and he will pray behind him.'"[84]

Sins and the Disobedience of Allah ﷻ

Whatever level and form of disobedience of Allah ﷻ that a person performs is to be considered as something major, however with that said, we must realize that not all sins are at the same level of

---

[84] *Al-Āmālī* of Shaykh Ṣadūq, Sitting (Majlis) 39, Tradition 4:

أَتَى يَهُودِيٌّ النَّبِيَّ ﷺ فَقَامَ بَيْنَ يَدَيْهِ يُحِدُّ النَّظَرَ إِلَيْهِ. فَقَالَ: يَا يَهُودِيُّ مَا حَاجَتُكَ؟ قَالَ: أَنْتَ أَفْضَلُ أَمْ مُوسَى بْنُ عِمْرَانَ النَّبِيُّ الَّذِي كَلَّمَهُ اللَّهُ وَأَنْزَلَ عَلَيْهِ التَّوْرَاةَ وَالْعَصَا وَفَلَقَ لَهُ الْبَحْرَ وَأَظَلَّهُ بِالْغَمَامِ؟ فَقَالَ لَهُ النَّبِيُّ ﷺ: إِنَّهُ يُكْرَهُ لِلْعَبْدِ أَنْ يُزَكِّيَ نَفْسَهُ وَلٰكِنِّي أَقُولُ إِنَّ آدَمَ (عليه السلام) لَمَّا أَصَابَ الْخَطِيئَةَ كَانَتْ تَوْبَتُهُ أَنْ قَالَ: اَللّٰهُمَّ إِنِّي أَسْأَلُكَ بِحَقِّ مُحَمَّدٍ وَآلِ مُحَمَّدٍ لَمَّا غَفَرْتَ لِي فَغَفَرَهَا اللّٰهُ لَهُ. وَإِنَّ نُوحًا لَمَّا رَكِبَ فِي السَّفِينَةِ وَخَافَ الْغَرَقَ قَالَ: اَللّٰهُمَّ إِنِّي أَسْأَلُكَ بِحَقِّ مُحَمَّدٍ وَآلِ مُحَمَّدٍ لَمَّا أَنْجَيْتَنِي مِنَ الْغَرَقِ فَنَجَّاهُ اللّٰهُ عَنْهُ. وَإِنَّ إِبْرَاهِيمَ (عليه السلام) لَمَّا أُلْقِيَ فِي النَّارِ قَالَ: اَللّٰهُمَّ إِنِّي أَسْأَلُكَ بِحَقِّ مُحَمَّدٍ وَآلِ مُحَمَّدٍ لَمَّا أَنْجَيْتَنِي مِنْهَا. فَجَعَلَهَا اللّٰهُ عَلَيْهِ بَرْدًا وَ سَلَامًا. وَإِنَّ مُوسَى (عليه السلام) لَمَّا أَلْقَى عَصَاهُ وَأَوْجَسَ فِي نَفْسِهِ خِيفَةً قَالَ: اَللّٰهُمَّ إِنِّي أَسْأَلُكَ بِحَقِّ مُحَمَّدٍ وَآلِ مُحَمَّدٍ لَمَّا آمَنْتَنِي. فَقَالَ اللّٰهُ جَلَّ جَلَالُهُ: لَا تَخَفْ إِنَّكَ أَنْتَ الْأَعْلَى. يَا يَهُودِيُّ! إِنَّ مُوسَى لَوْ أَدْرَكَنِي ثُمَّ لَمْ يُؤْمِنْ بِي وَبِنُبُوَّتِي مَا نَفَعَهُ إِيمَانُهُ شَيْئًا وَلَا نَفَعَتْهُ النُّبُوَّةُ! يَا يَهُودِيُّ وَمِنْ ذُرِّيَّتِي الْمَهْدِيُّ إِذَا خَرَجَ نَزَلَ عِيسَى بْنُ مَرْيَمَ لِنُصْرَتِهِ فَقَدَّمَهُ وَصَلَّى خَلْفَهُ.

severity. Some sins, such as lying, backbiting, or murder have a greater level of depravity associated with them and will entail a much more painful punishment in relation to other sins. In addition to this, the time when a sin is performed, the place in which it was committed, the intention of the sinner, one's knowledge or lack thereof regarding a sin, and whether a person continues to perform that sin or if it was a 'one-off' will all have an effect on the outcome and consequence of the sin.

The true worth of each person is measured in how much spiritual strength one has in the face of sins. A person that can resist sinning, has the greatest value in the sight of Allah ﷻ. In regard to this, Imam ʿAlī ؑ has been quoted as saying: "I swear by Allah that even if I am given the entire domain of the seven heavens in exchange for me to disobey Allah (and perform the sin) of taking one grain of barley from (the mouth of) an ant, I would never do so!"[85]

In addition, Imam ʿAlī ؑ also said: "The worst sin is that which the wrongdoer takes lightly."[86]

In another tradition we read: "Indeed the friends of (Prophet) Muḥammad are those who obey Allah even if they distanced from him (the Prophet) in genealogy; and indeed, the enemies of (Prophet) Muḥammad are those who disobey Allah even if they are closely related to him (the Prophet)."[87]

---

[85] *Nahj al-Balāgha*, Sermon 224 (222 in some versions).

[86] Ibid., Short Saying 477:

أَشَدُّ الذُّنُوبِ مَا اسْتَخَفَّ بِهِ صَاحِبُهُ.

[87] *Wasāʾil al-Shīʿa*, Vol. 15, Pg. 238:

إِنَّ وَلِيَّ مُحَمَّدٍ مَنْ أَطَاعَ اللَّهَ وَإِنْ بَعُدَتْ لُحْمَتُهُ وَإِنَّ عَدُوَّ مُحَمَّدٍ مَنْ عَصَى اللَّهَ وَإِنْ قَرُبَتْ قَرَابَتُهُ.

Converting a Minor Sin to a Major Sin

There are some actions and conditions [at the time of sinning] which can convert a minor sin into a major sin, some of which are the following:

1. Continuously performing minor sins.
2. Considering sins as being trivial.
3. Expressing joy and pleasure when committing a sin or after it.
4. Sinning by means of intentionally wanting to break the laws of Allah ﷻ.
5. Having pride and arrogance at the fact that Allah ﷻ gives His servants a reprieve when they sin (and does not punish them immediately).
6. Performing sins in the open.
7. Elderly people or individuals of a respectable status in society committing sins.

Different Effects of Sins

1. Hardness of the spiritual heart.
2. Removal of Divine blessings.
3. Rejection of one's supplications to Allah ﷻ.
4. Having one's sustenance constrained.
5. Being deprived from the ability to perform certain acts of worship, such as the Night Prayer *(Ṣalāt al-Layl).*
6. Unforeseen trials and tribulations.
7. Stoppage of Divine blessings such as rain.
8. Destruction of a person's property such as one's house.
9. Being plagued with scandals and humiliation in society.
10. Shortening of one's life span.

11. Earthquakes and natural disasters.
12. Poverty and destitution.
13. Grief and various other types of sicknesses.
14. Having wicked people take charge over them.

It must be noted that for each of these effects of sinning, there are verses of the Quran and *aḥādīth* which confirm them.

How to Recompense for Sins

1. The performance of *ṣalāt*: "And establish the prayer in the two parts of the day and in the first hours of the night; surely good deeds take away evil deeds. That is a reminder for the mindful."[88]
2. Asking forgiveness for oneself and for others *(shafāʿat)*: "And We did not send any Messenger but that he should be obeyed by the permission of Allah; and had they, when they were unjust to themselves, come to you (O Muḥammad) and asked for forgiveness from Allah, and the Messenger had (also) asked forgiveness for them, they would have found Allah Oft-returning (to Mercy), All-Merciful."[89]

---

[88] Quran, Sūrah Hūd (11), verse 114:

﴿وَأَقِمِ الصَّلَاةَ طَرَفَيِ النَّهَارِ وَزُلَفًا مِنَ اللَّيْلِ ۚ إِنَّ الْحَسَنَاتِ يُذْهِبْنَ السَّيِّئَاتِ ۚ ذَٰلِكَ ذِكْرَىٰ لِلذَّاكِرِينَ﴾

[89] Ibid., Sūrah al-Nisāʾ (4), verse 64:

﴿وَمَا أَرْسَلْنَا مِنْ رَسُولٍ إِلَّا لِيُطَاعَ بِإِذْنِ اللَّهِ ۚ وَلَوْ أَنَّهُمْ إِذْ ظَلَمُوا أَنْفُسَهُمْ جَاءُوكَ فَاسْتَغْفَرُوا اللَّهَ وَاسْتَغْفَرَ لَهُمُ الرَّسُولُ لَوَجَدُوا اللَّهَ تَوَّابًا رَحِيمًا﴾

3. Privately giving charity: "Charity given in secret becomes a penitence for one's sins."[90]
4. Helping to alleviate the challenges which others are facing in their lives: "From among the ways of the atonement for the major sins is to aide someone who is in a state of apprehension."[91]
5. Bringing about true faith and performing good deeds: "And (as for) those who believe and do righteous deeds, We will most certainly remove from them their evil deeds, and We will most certainly reward them the best of what they did."[92]
6. Keeping away from the major sins: "If you avoid the great sins which you are forbidden, We will remove from you your minor sins, and cause you to enter an honourable place of entering."[93]
7. Turning back to Allah ﷻ in repentance - *tawbah* - and making amends for the bad deeds performed: "Except for

---

[90] *Ghurur al-Ḥikm*:

صَدَقَةُ السِّرِّ تُكَفِّرُ الْخَطِيئَةَ.

[91] *Wasā'il al-Shī'a*, Vol. 16, Pg. 373:

مِنْ كَفَّارَاتِ الذُّنُوبِ الْعِظَامِ إِغَاثَةُ الْمَلْهُوفِ.

[92] Quran, Sūrah al-ʿAnkabūt (29), verse 7:

﴿وَالَّذِينَ آمَنُوا وَعَمِلُوا الصَّالِحَاتِ لَنُكَفِّرَنَّ عَنْهُمْ سَيِّئَاتِهِمْ وَلَنَجْزِيَنَّهُمْ أَحْسَنَ الَّذِي كَانُوا يَعْمَلُونَ﴾

[93] Ibid., Sūrah al-Nisā' (4), verse 31:

﴿إِنْ تَجْتَنِبُوا كَبَائِرَ مَا تُنْهَوْنَ عَنْهُ نُكَفِّرْ عَنْكُمْ سَيِّئَاتِكُمْ وَنُدْخِلْكُمْ مُدْخَلًا كَرِيمًا﴾

those who repent and believe and do righteous deeds; for those Allah will replace their evil deeds with good ones; and Allah is All-Forgiving, All-Merciful."[94]

8. Taking part in religiously ordained wars *(jihād)*, and attaining the rank of martyrdom *(shahādah)*: "So those who emigrated, or were evicted from their homes, or were persecuted in My way, or who fought and were slain, I will most certainly remove from them their evil deeds, and I will most certainly make them enter gardens beneath which rivers flow, as a reward from Allah, and with Allah is the best reward."[95]
9. Greeting others, feeding other people, and the performance of the Night Prayer *(Ṣalāt al-Layl)*: "There are three things which act as a penitence (for the sins that a person committed): spreading peace (greeting others with the commonly used phrase of *As-Salām ʿAlaykum* or *Salāmun ʿAlaykum*); feeding other people; and performing the Night Prayer while the rest of the people are asleep."[96]
10. The verbal declaration of *ṣalawāt* upon Muḥammad and the family of Muḥammad: "A person who is not able to

---

[94] Quran, Sūrah al-Furqān (25), verse 70:

﴿إِلَّا مَنْ تَابَ وَآمَنَ وَعَمِلَ عَمَلًا صَالِحًا فَأُولَٰئِكَ يُبَدِّلُ اللَّهُ سَيِّئَاتِهِمْ حَسَنَاتٍ ۗ وَكَانَ اللَّهُ غَفُورًا رَحِيمًا﴾

[95] Ibid., Sūrah Āle ʿImrān (3), verse 195:

﴿فَالَّذِينَ هَاجَرُوا وَأُخْرِجُوا مِنْ دِيَارِهِمْ وَأُوذُوا فِي سَبِيلِي وَقَاتَلُوا وَقُتِلُوا لَأُكَفِّرَنَّ عَنْهُمْ سَيِّئَاتِهِمْ وَلَأُدْخِلَنَّهُمْ جَنَّاتٍ تَجْرِي مِنْ تَحْتِهَا الْأَنْهَارُ ثَوَابًا مِنْ عِنْدِ اللَّهِ ۗ وَاللَّهُ عِنْدَهُ حُسْنُ الثَّوَابِ﴾

[96] *Wasāʾil al-Shīʿa*, Vol. 12, Pg. 59:

ثَلَاثٌ كَفَّارَاتٌ: إِفْشَاءُ السَّلَامِ، وَإِطْعَامُ الطَّعَامِ، وَالصَّلَاةُ بِاللَّيْلِ وَالنَّاسُ نِيَامٌ.

> gain deliverance from one's sins should make frequent prayers *(ṣalawāt)* upon Muḥammad and the family of Muḥammad, as this act destroys the sins - a complete destruction."[97]

The purification of the soul and self-accounting is different from counting the blessings of the Divine which one has been given. In verse 32 of the sūrah under review, Allah ﷻ clearly tells us: 'So do not acclaim your own virtue;' however in another place in the Quran, Allah ﷻ tells us: 'And as for the favour of your Lord, do announce (it).'[98]

Take Away Messages

1. We should point out the good people in a society by speaking about the good qualities that they possess.
2. The only time that the performance of good deeds carries any value is when they are accompanied with God-consciousness *(taqwā)* and one keeps away from sins.
3. Avoiding sins must become a way of life and be second nature for an individual; the usage of the present-tense verb in this verse in the word '*yajtanibūn*' - proves that this is something which is continuous and must always be present in the life of a person.

---

[97] *Biḥār al-Anwār*, Vol. 91, Pg. 47:

مَنْ لَمْ يَقْدِرْ عَلَىٰ مَا يُكَفِّرُ بِهِ ذُنُوبَهُ فَلْيُكْثِرْ مِنَ الصَّلَوَاتِ عَلَىٰ مُحَمَّدٍ وَآلِهِ فَإِنَّهَا تَهْدِمُ الذُّنُوبَ هَدْمًا.

[98] Quran, Sūrah al-Ḍhuḥā (93), verse 11:

﴿وَأَمَّا بِنِعْمَةِ رَبِّكَ فَحَدِّثْ ۝١١﴾

4. The clearest sign of good-doers is that they keep away from the major sins, and those sins which have a greater level of depravity in society.
5. Coming close to sins has the potential to pull a person closer to those sins, therefore the Quran uses the phrase of 'keeping away' from sins by saying 'those who **continuously keep away** from the major sins.'
6. People are not 'angels' on earth, and it is possible that even the best of people (except the Prophet ﷺ and his Ahlul Bayt ؑ) may make mistakes or even sin.
7. An ideal individual is one who hides the mistakes of other people and forgives their shortcomings.
8. Those sins which are committed in a moment of heedlessness and are not accompanied by any show of obstinacy or insistence on the part of the sinner should be overlooked and forgiven.
9. Being motivated when it comes to performing actions - whether good or bad - has various impacts on the performance of that deed. Therefore, those sins which do not stem from a desire to willfully transgress the laws and ordinances of Allah ﷻ are much more easily forgiven by Allah ﷻ compared to those sins which stem from a person's intended want and desire to break the laws of Allah ﷻ. Although all sins can be forgiven, however when a person makes a conscious decision to sin and knows what they are doing, such sins are much more difficult to seek pardon for from Allah ﷻ, and consequently are not as easily forgiven by Allah ﷻ as those done in a state of heedlessness.
10. The promise of having Divine forgiveness is not a reason or excuse for people to go on sinning - we must always try

and keep ourselves away from sins and help others to do the same.

11. Even those people who have performed major sins must never feel hopeless from the Mercy of Allah ﷻ.
12. Allah ﷻ has both Knowledge [of the sins] and Power [to punish], however He still often overlooks the sins which people perform.
13. Not only does Allah ﷻ know our "everything now," but He also knows the time when we were fetuses in the wombs of our mothers, so we must never be proud.
14. Those who keep away from sinning will not be prone to arrogance.
15. By paying attention to one's own mediocrity and past inabilities, an individual will be able to keep away from self-praise.
16. Improving a person's behaviour can be done through reforming one's religious beliefs. Having a strong belief in the Knowledge and Guardianship of Allah ﷻ will allow a human being to keep away from self-praise.
17. If we have any perfection within ourselves, it **all** stems from the Almighty One - how then can we ever be proud about anything?
18. By pretending to be God-conscious (one with *taqwā*), one will not become pious; rather a true and sincere effort must be made.

Part 12

The Deniers - Verses 33-37

أَفَرَءَيْتَ ٱلَّذِى تَوَلَّىٰ ﴿٣٣﴾ وَأَعْطَىٰ قَلِيلًا وَأَكْدَىٰٓ ﴿٣٤﴾ أَعِندَهُۥ عِلْمُ
ٱلْغَيْبِ فَهُوَ يَرَىٰٓ ﴿٣٥﴾ أَمْ لَمْ يُنَبَّأْ بِمَا فِى صُحُفِ مُوسَىٰ ﴿٣٦﴾ وَإِبْرَٰهِيمَ
ٱلَّذِى وَفَّىٰٓ ﴿٣٧﴾

33. Have you seen the one who turned away?

34. And gave a little, then held back?

35. Does he possess knowledge of the unseen, and can therefore foresee?

36. Or was he not informed about what was in the Scrolls of Mūsā?

37. And of Ibrāhīm, who fulfilled (his obligations)?

Thinking Points

The word *'akdā'* comes from the word *'kudyah'* which means 'miserliness and withholding one's hand from offering charity,' and its original meaning was 'ground that is hard.' The word *'waffa'* refers to 'always fulfilling one's obligations,' and has been used alongside Prophet Ibrāhīm (ʿa) because throughout his entire life, he was always faithful to the promises which he made.

Regarding the history of revelation of verse 33 [more specifically, this entire group of verses], it has been mentioned that they were revealed about an individual who used to assist needy people. When others saw him, they said to him: "If you continue helping others like this, a day will come when you yourself will become needy." Upon hearing this and thinking about it, he decided to stop helping the needy, and became miserly.

As this portion of the sūrah makes a direct note to Prophet Ibrāhīm ﷺ and him fulfilling his obligations, we note that when it comes to this great Prophet which Allah ﷻ sent, we see that the Quran praises him in many ways. Through the various verses, Allah ﷻ highlights some of his unique qualities, including the following:

1. Extremely patient *(awwāh)*
2. Submissive *(ḥalīm)*
3. One with insight *(baṣīr)*
4. Sincere *(mukhliṣ)*
5. Obedient *(qānat)*
6. Thankful *(shākir)*
7. Extremely truthful *(ṣiddīq)*
8. A true believer *(mo'min)*
9. One who performs beautiful actions *(muḥsin)*
10. Loyal *(wafī)*
11. A friend *(khalīl)*
12. A leader *(imām)*
13. An example for others to follow *(uswah)*
14. A nation on his own *(ummah)*,
15. devout worshipper *('ābid)*
16. An upright one *(ḥanīf)*
17. One who submits to Allah ﷻ

There are two instances in the Quran where Prophets Ibrāhīm ﷺ and Mūsā ﷺ have been mentioned alongside one another - one is in this chapter in the verses under review, and the other instance is found in the Quran where Allah ﷻ says: "The Scriptures of Ibrāhīm and Mūsā."[99]

Take Away Messages

1. When it comes to upbringing *(tarbiyah)*, we need to make use of proper role models and good examples which are around us.
2. When it comes to the daily activities and whatever a person performs, there must be a combination of an inclination towards that action, as well as a deep affinity for it. In addition, there must be a great deal of effort put into it, and it must be continuous. If any of these are missing, then it will be considered a flaw and defect. Through the Quranic usage of the word *'tawalla'* - 'turned away' we understand that it is problematic if a person does not have a tendency towards a specific action; and from the phrase *'a'ṭā qalīla'* - 'and gave a little,' we get the understanding of a person who did not put a great deal of effort into what they were required to perform; and from the word *'akdā'* - 'and held back' we realize that there should be continuity in the action.
3. When it comes to upbringing *(tarbiyah)* and trying to teach the good habits of a role model to someone, knowing the name of that person is not important - rather what is important is expressing the morals and qualities of that individual.

---

[99] Quran, Sūrah al-Aʿlā (87), verse 19:

﴿صُحُفِ إِبْرَاهِيمَ وَمُوسَىٰ﴾

4. Each of the two opposites of a human being - their spiritual ascension and spiritual decline - have multiple stages, however the initial stage is theological, and from there comes the practical (ascension or decline).
5. Someone who is poor and can only offer small amounts in charity is one who should be praised, as the Quran says: 'those who find nothing to give except (what they earn through) their hard toil;'[100] however those who have the financial means to give more but do not do so, then they are reprimanded in this chapter, as Allah ﷻ says: 'and gave a little.'
6. Sometimes, providing minimal assistance is a wise decision, such as when someone gives a small amount of food to a child because if a person was to give too much food to a child, then it would be detrimental to the child's health, or it would be wasted and thrown out. However, sometimes the giving of a small amount by someone to a needy person is done because that person is stingy, and this is what has been reproached in the Quran.
7. One of the ways to cure the sickness of stinginess is to remember those people [of the past and present] who are generous and self-sacrificing.
8. A person does not know whether in the future they may fall into poverty, such that today they maintain stinginess [thinking that there is a possibility that they may become poor later so they do not give anything to charity now].

---

[100] Quran, Sūrah al-Tawbah (9), verse 79:

﴿ٱلَّذِينَ يَلْمِزُونَ ٱلْمُطَّوِّعِينَ مِنَ ٱلْمُؤْمِنِينَ فِى ٱلصَّدَقَٰتِ وَٱلَّذِينَ لَا يَجِدُونَ إِلَّا جُهْدَهُمْ فَيَسْخَرُونَ
مِنْهُمْ سَخِرَ ٱللَّهُ مِنْهُمْ وَلَهُمْ عَذَابٌ أَلِيمٌ ٧٩﴾

9. Although we believe that the previous Divinely-revealed Scriptures have been tampered with, there are still some areas which we can refer to in those books.
10. The Divinely-revealed teachings of the past Prophets all share some similar principles.
11. It is through mentioning the names of the past revered people and their accomplishments and services that we can honour them.
12. When it comes to propagation *(tablīgh)* and guidance of others, we should always make use of examples which everyone agrees upon. In this case we see that Allah ﷻ used the names of two great Prophets - Mūsā ؑ and Ibrāhīm ؑ - as they were well-known to the Arabs at the time of the appointment of Prophet Muḥammad ﷺ.
13. Regarding upbringing *(tarbiyah)*, we must present examples from both ends of the spectrum - positive and negative ones.
14. One of the greatest perfections of the human character is to be loyal on the path of the truth.

Part 13

What You Deserve - Verses 38-41

أَلَّا تَزِرُ وَازِرَةٌ وِزْرَ أُخْرَىٰ ﴿٣٨﴾ وَأَن لَّيْسَ لِلْإِنسَٰنِ إِلَّا مَا سَعَىٰ ﴿٣٩﴾
وَأَنَّ سَعْيَهُۥ سَوْفَ يُرَىٰ ﴿٤٠﴾ ثُمَّ يُجْزَىٰهُ ٱلْجَزَآءَ ٱلْأَوْفَىٰ ﴿٤١﴾

38. That no soul shall bear the burden of another soul.

39. And there is not for the human being except what one strives for.

40. And one's efforts will be witnessed.

41. Then one will be rewarded for it the fullest reward.

Thinking Points

Verses 38 to 54 present the teachings which are found in the Books of Prophets Ibrāhīm ﷺ and Mūsā ﷺ that are also accepted in the religion of Islam.

The word '*wizr*' refers to 'a heavy load' and can also be used for sins, which are a heavy burden that a person carries. The word '*wazīr*' refers to 'a person who has taken on the weighty responsibility of running the affairs of a country.'

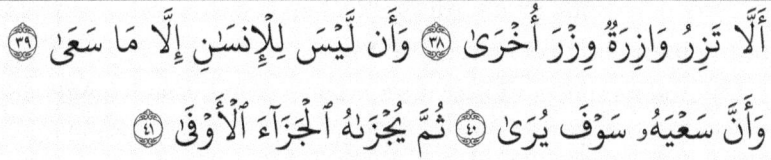

Through one's good actions, Allah ﷻ has promised to erase the bad deeds which a person performs; or through a person's turning back to Allah ﷻ *(tawbah)* and seeking forgiveness from Him *(istighfār)*, He will forgive them; or He will transform their bad deeds into good deeds. However, He will never unfairly place the burden of the sins of one person onto the shoulders of another person.

When the second caliph, ʿUmar ibn al-Khaṭṭāb, gave the order that a pregnant woman who had committed adultery *(zinā)* should be stoned to death, Imam ʿAlī ﷺ stood up and said: "What sin has her unborn fetus committed?" By relying upon the verse which says: 'And no soul shall bear the burden of another soul' the Imam ﷺ went on to say: "Be patient until she delivers her baby, and then carry out your penalty upon her."[101]

The Noble Prophet ﷺ has been quoted as saying: "The sin of the couple who committed adultery *(zinā)* does not fall on the shoulders of the child born out of wedlock," then he recited the verse of the Quran which reads: 'And no soul shall bear the burden of another soul.'[102]

At this point, a question may arise that: In the verse of this chapter, it says: 'And there is not for the human being except what one strives for,' however in other verses of the Quran and in the *aḥādīth* we read that 'sometimes a person may enter Paradise through the intercession of others *(shafāʿat)*.' Thus, it appears that there is a contradiction here: Is it through one's own deeds that a person will be rewarded with Paradise, or can others intercede and take a person to Heaven?

The response to this question is multi-faceted:

First off: This verse sought to remove the ignorant *(jahlī)* concept that people used to have in which they would say to one another: If you give me a certain amount of money, I will take the responsibility and burden of your sins on my shoulders. The Quran came to nullify such a belief and tell the people that: 'No one can

---

[101] *Biḥār al-Anwār*, Vol. 76, Pg. 49.

[102] *Tafsīr Rāhnumā* and *Tafsīr al-Durr al-Manthūr.*

take the burden of sins for another person, and everyone will only get what one strives for.'

Secondly: This verse gives us a glimpse into the Justice *('Adl)* of Allah ﷻ, not the Grace *(Faḍhl)* of Allah ﷻ - meaning that according to His Justice, the punishments and rewards of each person are based on the amount of their efforts. However, Allah ﷻ can through His Grace, bestow His Benevolence and give a greater reward to an individual or reduce a person's retribution - as He says in the Quran that 'and give them more out of His Grace.'[103]

Thirdly: When we see that it has been mentioned in the traditions that: "If an individual establishes either a praiseworthy or an immoral tradition *(sunnah)* in the community, they will share in the rewards or retributions of everyone who followed that particular action which they established," then this definitely does not go against the verse which reads: 'And there is not for the human being except what one strives for' - as the one who established the path of truth or falsehood is also by means of acting as an intermediary, a proof and guide to that action, or can be considered as one who initiated the prerequisites and laid down that which was required for that action to perpetuate in society, or was the one who was able to propagate and encourage, or contribute in any other way - either materially or psychologically - and was able to indirectly exert some level of effort. Thus, for such a person to receive some of the rewards or punishments for their actions is not something baseless, just as if a person did not

---

[103] Quran, Sūrah al-Nisā' (4), verse 173:

﴿فَأَمَّا ٱلَّذِينَ ءَامَنُوا۟ وَعَمِلُوا۟ ٱلصَّٰلِحَٰتِ فَيُوَفِّيهِمْ أُجُورَهُمْ وَيَزِيدُهُم مِّن فَضْلِهِۦ ۖ وَأَمَّا ٱلَّذِينَ ٱسْتَنكَفُوا۟ وَٱسْتَكْبَرُوا۟ فَيُعَذِّبُهُمْ عَذَابًا أَلِيمًا وَلَا يَجِدُونَ لَهُم مِّن دُونِ ٱللَّهِ وَلِيًّا وَلَا نَصِيرًا ١٧٣﴾

walk the correct path in life, there is no way that such a person would be worthy of having intercession *(shafāʿat)* to assist them.

We read in the traditions that after death, a person will benefit from the righteous actions of one's child, or from a book (of knowledge), or something else that one bequeathed which others benefit from.[104] We also read in a verse of the Quran that in Paradise, a person's righteous children will be in one's company.[105] Finally, in some narrations it says that if a person encourages others to do good deeds, then after one's death, if people perform those actions, then that individual (who encouraged others) will also receive rewards for that which was done.[106]

In all of these instances, although the individual did not directly exhort any efforts, but one was indirectly involved in it - for example, the proper upbringing of one's child who stayed on the path of righteousness, or a person who leaves something behind as an endowment, or one who assisted in some Islamic literature which others benefited from, or an individual imparted some good advice which others went on to follow in their lives - then even

---

[104] *Al-Khiṣāl*, Pg. 151.

[105] Quran, Sūrah al-Ṭūr (52), verse 21:

﴿وَٱلَّذِينَ ءَامَنُوا۟ وَٱتَّبَعَتْهُمْ ذُرِّيَّتُهُم بِإِيمَٰنٍ أَلْحَقْنَا بِهِمْ ذُرِّيَّتَهُمْ وَمَآ أَلَتْنَٰهُم مِّنْ عَمَلِهِم مِّن شَىْءٍ ۚ كُلُّ ٱمْرِئٍۭ بِمَا كَسَبَ رَهِينٌ ۝٢١﴾

Those who have believed and their offspring have followed them in faith, We will unite them with their offspring (even though the faith of the latter may not be of the same degree as that of the former), and We will not decrease the reward of their deeds in anything (because of their being united with their offspring). Every person will enjoy according to what he has earned.

[106] *Al-Kāfī*, Vol. 4, Pg. 315.

after a person's death, the deceased will share in the rewards of those worthy actions because they had played some role in them.

Take Away Messages

1. The retributions and rewards of Allah ﷻ are all distributed justly.
2. Do not afflict yourself with sins, thinking that you can rely on others to help you out as they will never be able to be responsible for carrying the burden of your sins.
3. In the appointment or dismissal of individuals to positions, never allow relatives or those close to you to influence your decision.
4. This world is the field of putting forth efforts and working hard, and to some extent you will see the outcome of your actions.
5. We are obliged to perform our duties, but we are not responsible for achieving perfect results - we are only responsible to do the best that we can do.
6. When it comes to a person's actions, having a belief that the effects of them will continue to exist, and that there is a just system of punishment and reward (of Allah ﷻ) - can encourage and inspire a person to act in the right way; and at the same time, it will instill caution and restraint in the individual.
7. No actions that are performed in this world are ever lost or destroyed.
8. People who perform good actions are never in a hurry to receive their rewards (because they know that it will not be overlooked or forgotten with Allah ﷻ.

9. This transient world does not have the capacity to provide a full recompense for all the deeds that people perform, therefore there must exist something called the Day of Judgement for everyone to get full compensation for their actions.
10. The good actions of a person are rewarded with even better rewards (than one ever expected to receive).
11. Although there are some punishments in this world for bad deeds, full retribution can only take place in the hereafter.
12. The resurrection has several stages and sojourns, and from the usage of the word *'sawfa'* - 'soon,' and the word *'thumma'* - 'then at that point,' we can deduce that the levels of witnessing the actions will be different from the stages of retributions for the actions.

Part 14

The True Lord - Verses 42-44

وَأَنَّ إِلَىٰ رَبِّكَ ٱلْمُنتَهَىٰ ﴿٤٢﴾ وَأَنَّهُۥ هُوَ أَضْحَكَ وَأَبْكَىٰ ﴿٤٣﴾ وَأَنَّهُۥ هُوَ
أَمَاتَ وَأَحْيَا ﴿٤٤﴾

42. And that to your Lord is the finality,

43. And that it is He who causes laughter and weeping,

44. And that it is He who gives death and life.

Thinking Points

Although the acts which Allah ﷻ performs are sometimes through an intermediary, all actions stem from Him. The repetition of the pronoun '*huwa*' meaning 'Him' (Allah ﷻ) shows that all actions in this world belong to and emanate from Allah ﷻ.

The contrast between laughter and weeping, and death and life, are all things which human beings experience. In the presence of Allah ﷻ, all these things are good in their own way, and there is really no conflict between them.

Take Away Messages

1. Neither do the believers get tired of submitting to Allah ﷻ and performing what they are required to do as His servants, nor do the willfully-ignorant deniers of Allah ﷻ ever get tired of remaining proud for whatever reasons they are arrogant - except that the result for everything is

in the hands of Allah ﷻ, and He will take everyone to account for what they performed in the life of this world.

2. Everyone and everything are on the move towards Him.
3. Both the punishments and rewards are all in His hands, just as Allah ﷻ says 'soon shall you all see.' In addition, the moods and feelings of sorrow and joy which we feel are also in His hands.
4. Laughing and crying are both necessary in life, thus when a person is going through different emotional states, one should not be prevented from expressing their sentiments.
5. The Power of Allah ﷻ regarding actions and their consequences is equal.
6. The Day of Judgement will be a day of laughter for some, and a day of crying for others - depending on their actions in this world.
7. Death and life are both manifestations of Divine Mercy.
8. The method of training which the Quran makes use of is that even when it is speaking about opposites, it still seeks to instill within the readers the issue of Monotheism *(Tawḥīd)*.

Part 15

Some of the Powers of Allah - Verses 45-49

وَأَنَّهُۥ خَلَقَ ٱلزَّوْجَيْنِ ٱلذَّكَرَ وَٱلْأُنثَىٰ ﴿٤٥﴾ مِن نُّطْفَةٍ إِذَا تُمْنَىٰ ﴿٤٦﴾ وَأَنَّ
عَلَيْهِ ٱلنَّشْأَةَ ٱلْأُخْرَىٰ ﴿٤٧﴾ وَأَنَّهُۥ هُوَ أَغْنَىٰ وَأَقْنَىٰ ﴿٤٨﴾ وَأَنَّهُۥ هُوَ رَبُّ
ٱلشِّعْرَىٰ ﴿٤٩﴾

45. And that it is He who created the two kinds - the male and the female.

46. From a sperm drop when it is emitted.

47. And that upon Him is the next existence.

48. And that it is He who enriches and impoverishes.

49. And that it is He who is the Lord of Sirius.

Thinking Points

The word '*aghnā*' comes from the root word '*ghinā*' and it means 'to be needless;' the word '*aqnā*' comes from the root word '*qunyah*' and it means 'to save one's wealth,'[107] however there are

---

[107] *Al-Mufradāt.*

some scholars who have stated that this word means 'to make someone poor.'[108]

When commenting on the verse from this section which reads: 'And that it is He who enriches and impoverishes,' Imam 'Alī said the following: "Allah not only makes people free from need (by enriching them), but He is the same Entity who also makes people happy by providing them with wealth."[109]

The word 'al-shi'rā' is the name of a star (Sirius) which a group of people used to worship as they thought that this star had a role to play in their poverty and prosperity. In response, the Quran is basically answering them by saying: "That star is under the control of Allah, and it has no role to play in your lives."

In addition, there are some who considered that the word 'al-shi'rā' was the name of one of the idols which some people worshipped.[110]

The pairing of the genders (male and female) as mentioned in this passage is the secret towards the survival of humanity (through them having children), and if this phenomenon of mates were to be removed then life would become cold and lonely, and the existence of creations on this planet as we know it, would end.

Take Away Messages

1. The law of pairs (of a male and female) is something which Allah placed in the system of creation in this universe,

---

[108] *Al-Qāmūs al-Quran.*

[109] *Tafsir al-Qummī.*

[110] *Tafsīr Nemunah.*

and it is not something which human beings determined on their own amongst themselves.

2. The implementation of the contradictory designs on a material element is a sign of the Power and Glory of Allah ﷻ - as Allah ﷻ indicates in this chapter with phrases like 'laughing and crying,' 'death and life,' and 'male and female.'
3. The creation of the male and female is both from the wonders of the creations of Allah ﷻ, as well as a necessity for life to exist.
4. A man and woman are made from the same element of creation.
5. Just as Allah ﷻ can create a living creature from a single drop of sperm, similarly He is also able to resurrect the creation once they have been reduced to mere dead particles in the earth.
6. It is necessary for Allah ﷻ to revive the dead, then begin the process of resurrection.
7. It is Allah ﷻ who originates the creation, and it is also Him who creates the variety which is seen in creation. He created pairs (the male and female) which exist in the world of creation, and it is also He who ensures that the sperm which He created continues to exist. It is also Allah ﷻ who is responsible for overseeing the creation of everything today, and even tomorrow, and in the future it will still be Him who will be in charge for all of eternity.
8. We must seek to be free from need by asking for everything from Him alone, and not from the creations.
9. Now that it is understood that being needy and free from want is all in His hands, why do people still insist on being

stingy, having pride, and seeking their needs from other than Him?

10. The preservation which Allah ﷻ provides is given to a fetus in the womb of its mother, and it is also given to a star in the sky.

Part 16

Previous Nations - Verses 50-56

وَأَنَّهُۥٓ أَهۡلَكَ عَادًا ٱلۡأُولَىٰ ﴿٥٠﴾ وَثَمُودَاْ فَمَآ أَبۡقَىٰ ﴿٥١﴾ وَقَوۡمَ نُوحٖ مِّن
قَبۡلُۖ إِنَّهُمۡ كَانُواْ هُمۡ أَظۡلَمَ وَأَطۡغَىٰ ﴿٥٢﴾ وَٱلۡمُؤۡتَفِكَةَ أَهۡوَىٰ ﴿٥٣﴾ فَغَشَّىٰهَا
مَا غَشَّىٰ ﴿٥٤﴾ فَبِأَيِّ ءَالَآءِ رَبِّكَ تَتَمَارَىٰ ﴿٥٥﴾ هَٰذَا نَذِيرٞ مِّنَ ٱلنُّذُرِ
ٱلۡأُولَىٰٓ ﴿٥٦﴾

50. And that it is He who destroyed the first ʿĀd.

51. And Thamūd, sparing no one.

52. And the people of Nūḥ before that; for they were most unjust and most oppressive.

53. And He toppled the ruined cities,

54. And covered them with whatever He covered them.

55. So which of the favours of your Lord do you doubt?

56. This is a warning, just like the previous warnings.

Thinking Points

The word *'mu'tafikah'* comes from the word *'i'tifāk'* and means 'something which has been turned upside down' or 'something which has been obliterated.' Since the cities where the community of ʿĀd lived were turned upside down due to the punishment which they received, it is for this reason that this specific word was chosen to describe their outcome.

The word *'ahwā'* means 'to fall' or 'to sink;' while the word *'tatamārā'* means 'to argue with someone else accompanied by a sense of doubt and misgiving (in the other person).'

As for the portion of this verse which reads: "For they were most unjust and most oppressive" it is very well possible that this was in regards to the nation of Prophet Nūḥ ﵇ who were even more oppressive than ʿĀd and Thamūd; but it is also possible that it could be in regards to the nations of ʿĀd, Thamūd, and Nūḥ ﵇ all together - meaning that in comparison to all of the other communities which have been destroyed over time, these three were the most unjust and oppressive.

Take Away Messages

1. Punishments (from Allah ﷻ) are not only reserved for the world to come; rather Allah ﷻ destroyed some communities in the life of this world as well.
2. We must do our best to take lessons from the vicious outcomes and destructions of the previous deviant nations.
3. Injustice and oppression - especially continuing to go down that route - are the sources of one's downfall.
4. When it comes to studying history, its events, and the changes which occur therein, we must always pay attention to the reasons behind what transpired.
5. One of the blessings and graces of the Divine is the fact that oppressors are often destroyed right here in the life of this world.
6. The main responsibility of all the Prophets ﵈ and the Divinely-revealed Books is to warn and advise people.

Part 17

Submit to Allah - Verses 57-62

أَزِفَتِ ٱلْءَازِفَةُ ﴿٥٧﴾ لَيْسَ لَهَا مِن دُونِ ٱللَّهِ كَاشِفَةٌ ﴿٥٨﴾ أَفَمِنْ هَٰذَا
ٱلْحَدِيثِ تَعْجَبُونَ ﴿٥٩﴾ وَتَضْحَكُونَ وَلَا تَبْكُونَ ﴿٦٠﴾ وَأَنتُمْ سَٰمِدُونَ
﴿٦١﴾ فَٱسْجُدُوا۟ لِلَّهِ وَٱعْبُدُوا۟ ۩ ﴿٦٢﴾

57. The inevitable is imminent.

58. None besides Allah can unveil it.

59. Do you marvel at this discourse?

60. And laugh, and do not weep?

61. And are lost in your frivolity?

62. So bow down to Allah, and worship!

Thinking Points

The word '*āzifa*' means 'approaching,' while the word '*sāmid*' refers to 'forgetfulness, inattention, and pride.'

In a *ḥadīth* which has been reported in *Tafsīr al-Furqān,* we read that from the point of revelation of these verses until the end of his life, the Noble Prophet ﷺ was never seen laughing - he only smiled (when the need arose).

It must also be noted that by reading or listening to the final verse of this chapter, one **must** perform an obligatory prostration *(sajdah).*

It is possible that the meaning of the phrase 'this discourse' is the Quran itself, just as was mentioned in verse 23 of Sūrah al-Zumar (39) in which the Quran is also referred to as a '*ḥadīth*' where Allah ﷻ says: "Allah sent down the best discourse."

Take Away Messages

1. Do not consider the Day of Judgement to be something far away.
2. All the means and ways [which a person feels that they can make use of] can never even reduce a small iota of the difficulties of resurrection.
3. Given that there are so many proofs around us for a physical resurrection on the Day of Judgement, and this is something which all the Prophets sent by Allah ﷻ also preached about, it is astonishing to see that there are some people who are surprised to hear that there will be a Day of Resurrection.
4. Those who truly believe in resurrection should reduce their laughter and fall more into the remembrance of the Day of Resurrection.
5. Sometimes laughter can be a symbol of pride and arrogance.
6. One of the best ways to treat pride and arrogance is to fall into the prostration *(sajdah)* of Allah ﷻ, and to engage in the worship of Him.

Other Publications Available[1]

1. *A Land Most Goodly: The Story of Yemen in the Quran and in the Times of Prophet Muḥammad and Imam ʿAlī ibn Abī Ṭālib* by Jaffer Ladak
2. *A Star Amongst the Stars: The life and times of the great companion: Jabir ibn Abdullah al-Ansari* by Jaffer Ladak
3. *Alif, Baa, Taa of Kerbala* by Saleem Bhimji, and Arifa Hudda
4. *Arbāʿīn of Imam Ḥusayn* compiled and translated by Saleem Bhimji
5. *Contentious Issues in Islamic History - ʿUmar ibn al-Khaṭṭāb* written by Saʿīd Dāwarī and translated by Saleem Bhimji
6. *Deficient? A Review of Sermon 80 from Nahj al-Balāgha* by Āyatullāh al-ʿUẓmā Shaykh Nāṣir Makārim Shīrāzī and translated by Saleem Bhimji
7. *Exegesis of the 29th Juz of the Quran - a translation of Tafsīr Namuneh* by Āyatullāh al-ʿUẓmā Shaykh Nāṣir Makārim Shīrāzī and translated by Saleem Bhimji
8. *Foundations of Islamic Unity* - a translation of *Al-Fuṣūl Al-Muhimmah fī Ta'līf al-Ummah* by ʿAbd al-Ḥusayn Sharaf al-Dīn al-Mūsawī al-ʿĀmilī and translated by Batool Ispahany

---

[1] The following is a list of all original writings and translations from the Islamic Publishing House. As many of these titles are out of stock, we are re-releasing all our works via Print-on-Demand through Amazon.

Search for the title that you are looking for via Amazon on one of their international platforms, including: Australia, Canada, France, Germany, Italy, Japan, UK, USA, Netherlands, and Spain.

If you cannot find any of the above titles on Amazon, feel free to email us at *iph@iph.ca*.

9. *Fountain of Paradise - Fāṭima az-Zahrā'* ﷺ *in the Noble Quran* by Āyatullāh al-'Uẓmā Shaykh Nāṣir Makārim Shīrāzī, compiled and translated by Saleem Bhimji
10. *God and god of Science* by Syed Hasan Raza Jafri
11. *House of Sorrows* by Shaykh 'Abbās al-Qummī and translated by Aejaz Ali Turab Husayn Husayni
12. *Inspirational Insights* by Mohammed Khaku
13. *Islam and Religious Pluralism* by Āyatullāh Shaykh Murtaḍā Muṭahharī and translated by Sayyid Sulayman Ali Hasan
14. *Journey to Eternity - A Handbook of Supplications for the Soul* compiled and translated by Saleem Bhimji and Arifa Hudda
15. *Living The Quran Through The Living Quran: Sūrah al-Najm - A Translation of Tafsīr Nūr* by Shaykh Muḥsin Qarā'atī and translated by Saleem Bhimji
16. *Living The Quran Through The Living Quran: Sūrah Qāf - A Translation of Tafsīr Nūr* by Shaykh Muḥsin Qarā'atī and translated by Saleem Bhimji
17. *Love and Hate for Allah's Sake* by Mujtabā Ṣabūrī translated by Saleem Bhimji
18. *Love for the Family* compiled and translated by Yasin T. Al-Jibouri, Saleem Bhimji, and others
19. *Moral Management* by 'Abbās Raḥīmī and translated by Saleem Bhimji
20. *Morals of the Masumeen* by Arifa Hudda
21. *Prayers of the Final Prophet - A collection of supplications of Prophet Muḥammad* by 'Allāmah Sayyid Muḥammad Ḥusayn Ṭabā'ṭabā'ī and translated by Tahir Ridha-Jaffer
22. *Ramaḍān Reflections* compiled by A Group of Muslim Scholars and translated by Saleem Bhimji
23. *Ṣalāt al-Āyāt* by Saleem Bhimji

24. *Ṣalāt al-Ghufaylah: Salvation through Patience & Perseverance* written by Saleem Bhimji
25. *Secrets of the Ḥajj* by Āyatullāh al-ʿUẓmā Shaykh Ḥusayn Mazāherī and translated by Saleem Bhimji
26. *Sunan an-Nabī* by ʿAllāmah Sayyid Muḥammad Ḥusayn Ṭabāʾṭabāʾī and translated by Tahir Ridha-Jaffer
27. *Tears from Heaven's Flowers: An Anthology of English Poetry about the Ahlulbayt* by Abrahim al-Zubeidi
28. *The Firmest Armament: Commentary on Āyatul Kursī (The Verse of the Throne)* by Sayyid Naṣrullāh Burujerdī and translated by Saleem Bhimji
29. *The Last Luminary and Ways to Delve into the Light* by Sayyid Muḥammad Riḍā Ḥusaynī Muṭlaq and translated by Saleem Bhimji
30. *The Muslim Legal Will Booklet* by Saleem Bhimji
31. *The Pure Life* by Āyatullāh al-ʿUẓmā as-Sayyid Muḥammad Taqī al-Modarresī and translated by Jaffer Ladak with commentary by Dr. Zainali Panjwani and Jaffer Ladak
32. *The Third Testimony: Imam ʿAlī in the Adhān* compiled and translated by Saleem Bhimji
33. *The Torch of Perpetual Guidance - A Brief Commentary on Ziyārat al-ʿĀshūrāʾ* by ʿAbbās ʿAzīzī and translated by Saleem Bhimji
34. *The Tragedy of Karbalāʾ by Imam ʿAlī ibn al-Ḥusayn as-Sajjād and translated by ʿAbdul-Zahrāʾ ʿAbdul-Ḥussain*
35. *Weapon of the Believer* by ʿAllāmah Muḥammad Bāqir Majlisī and translated by Saleem Bhimji

In addition to these titles which are currently available, look for our series of booklets featuring the commentary of the Noble Quran entitled *Living the Quran Through The Living Quran - A Translation of Tafsīr Nūr* of Shaykh Muḥsin Qarā'atī. This series of booklets will be available exclusively from Amazon.

www.ingramcontent.com/pod-product-compliance
Lightning Source LLC
Chambersburg PA
CBHW051351040426
42453CB00025B/280
* 9 7 8 1 9 2 7 9 3 0 4 5 8 *